Hasnain Waris has brought a lot of thought, scholarship, and heart into this engrossing book on the path of the Sufi, which is love. In simple and clear terms, the book gives us a comprehensive perspective of the philosophy and practice of Sufism, at the heart of which is the quest for the Beloved or supreme consciousness. Illustrating his points with delightful Sufi stories and thought-provoking excerpts from Rumi and other Sufi saints, while weaving in the scientific view, the book leads us through the journey travelled by the Sufi to reach the perfection he is in search of. In Sufi terms, the journey begins with moving from *nafs-e-ammara* (the animal self) to *nafs-e-kamila* (the perfect self).

I enjoyed this intimate and informed book and have locked away in my heart a few stories and insights the book gifted me.

— Suma Varughese
Founder-Facilitator of The Zen of
Good Writing Course and Former Editor of *Life
Positive* and *Society* magazines

In *S for Sufi*, Hasnain Waris has introduced the path of a Sufi in the simplest possible way with the help of daily objects like fruits, Hindu, Buddhist, and Bhakti chants, and even tales of Mulla Nasruddin. The resultant book is a breezy memorable walk through the archways of Sufi mysticism. Hasnain has conceived the book in the most interesting way by introducing the fundamentals of Sufism without resorting to any complex narration. The author's words have a voice, and the reader will be able to hear him speak through the pages. A mesmerising and outstanding book that interested readers must not miss.

— Kallol Bhattacherjee
Author and Journalist

S FOR SUFI

A Beginner's Guide *to* Sufi Spirituality

Hasnain Waris

Hay House Publishers India

Australia • India

United Kingdom • United States

Hay House Publishers (India) Pvt. Ltd.
Muskaan Complex, Plot No.3, B-2 Vasant Kunj, New Delhi-110 070, India
Hay House Inc., PO Box 5100, Carlsbad, CA 92018-5100, USA
Hay House UK, Ltd., The Sixth Floor, Watson House, 54 Baker Street, W1U 7BU, UK
Hay House Australia Pty Ltd., 18/36 Ralph St., Alexandria NSW 2015, Australia

Email: contact@hayhouse.co.in
www.hayhouse.co.in

ISBN 978-93-91067-28-1
ISBN 978-93-91067-33-5 (e-book)

Printed at Repro India Limited

Dedicated to my murshid
Hazrat Roshan Shah Warsi (R.A.), my source
of 'Light'. To my mother for introducing me
to my murshid. To my father who
never interfered in my eccentric spiritual quest.
To my family that stood by me
through it all.

Contents

Introduction

Stuck in the traffic driving back home from the office one day, I received a call from an unknown number. Thinking it would help me while away my time in the jam, I answered the phone on impulse. The person at the other end, who sounded like an educated man in his early thirties, said, "Good evening sir. I am a life coach and speaker. I was transported by your talk on 'Love and its transformative power'. It was a moving experience! I am a big fan of Sufism. I go to Hazrat Nizamuddin's dargah and have been to Ajmer Sharif many a time . . . and Coke studio . . . Sain Zahoor . . . Nusrat Fateh Ali Khan . . . these shrines are such peaceful places, I tell you! I vouch for their miraculous powers." He gushed all this in the same breath. I knew what was coming next! "If all efforts at lifting one's life condition are failing, one should try these places. But mind you, one has to be regular for at least seven Thursdays. And the evening *qawwalis*—they are just out of the world!"

This is what I hear every other day from friends who know a little about my Sufi bent and have bought into the Sufi fad that seems to have taken the world by storm. I wondered what the caller's real motive was in calling me. There had to be something more than this PR exercise. Just as I was thinking this, pat came the question, "Sir could you recommend a nice Sufi restaurant in central Delhi? I wish to take my girlfriend out this weekend." Sufi restaurant? The question surprised and upset me at the same time. I replied in a hurry, as if to cut the conversation short and focus on the traffic ahead, "Sorry, I don't know of any such place. Please Google." He seemed a little letdown and surprised at my brusqueness. I could sense that my indifferent response had put him off. How come a Sufi spiritual coach didn't know anything about Sufi recreational places in town? He politely agreed to Google the place and go by the recommendations and online reviews left by diners. Even before he might have Googled, I started typing 'Sufi restaurants in Delhi' and was inundated with a plethora of results which included Sufiana in Rajouri Garden, Faqiri—Sufi cafe and couture, Hotel Sufi, and Sufi nights. Curiosity compelled me to prod a little further, even though I dreaded the results. I removed the word 'Delhi' from the search, and, no longer to my surprise, found Sufi restaurants, cafes, and bars in almost all the big cities of the world from Kabul to San Diego, London to Bangalore.

This incident got me thinking. It was hard for me to believe that people are trivialising something so sublime. In fact, they are turning on its head the whole concept of Sufi—from losing the sense of self into pleasuring of the senses! To me, the individual is not wrong; he is the victim of a system and a society which privileges material aspirations and degrades anything and everything in pursuit of sensual gratification. A society that has accepted emotional charges and thrills as the ultimate goal of human existence. In times where all spiritual paths have been diluted by rituals, entertainment, superstitions, culturalism, mellowed extremism, and a transactional attitude, then how can Sufism remain untainted by this downward trend.

After this incident, I resolved to write the book you are holding in your hand right now, in order to explain the true spirit of Sufism to genuine seekers. With my own limited capacity and experience, I aim to explain Sufism's uniqueness and bring to readers its transformative side and hope to familiarise them with this core aspect of Sufism that has taken a back seat in present times, especially in the eastern world.

Author's Note

Dear reader, thank you for picking up this book. I appreciate your interest in the subject. You might have heard of certain analogies in scriptures and folklore such as when two water bodies meet, the dead comes back to life. What is the meaning hidden in this symbolism? What happens when the two water bodies meet? To my understanding, the two water bodies here refer to the eternal truth and contemporary interpretation, and so, when they meet, the dead wisdom gets a new lease of life. All our scriptures and classic spiritual texts are full of analogies and symbolism. And most of them talk in ancient languages, which might be no longer used by a contemporary man. Back then, these metaphors served the purpose of putting the reader in a reflective mode and inviting them to read between the lines and explore things beyond what meets the eye. But over these years, partly because of the evolution of language and partly because of a literal interpretation of these analogies and metaphors, the reader of these marvellous literary masterpieces might miss out the reason for which they were initially intended—developing human capacity. On the contrary, most people today interpret them in their own way with very little understanding of the language. This interpretation is further hampered by ego and conditioning. Most often they read the translations of these scriptures which fail to give similar parallels to the original metaphors or idioms. Or in other words, the real message gets lost in the translation.

Consequently, they try to interpret the thousands of year old psychological tips literally and struggle to absorb and apply them relevantly. These pedantic followers at best can read these books but fail to read between the lines and understand what these scriptures are trying to teach them. Coupled with their ego, this lack of understanding renders them into fanatics and hardliners who keep on uttering the right verses but with the wrong actions.

The reason behind a lot of regression and fall of standards in moral-based societies is this literalism which is, unfortunately, increasing at an alarming rate. People are ready to die for their religion or cult they don't understand and never actually practice or benefit from. No wonder these societies which are dominated by great numbers of such individuals are ideal breeding grounds for both superstition and extremism. Going by what they see happening around them in the name of spirituality or religion, the rationalists, especially the younger generation, either show very little interest in the practices of their fathers and ancestors or follow their rituals like habits without knowing the real meaning and purpose behind what they are doing. Also, thanks to our liberal society, some even openly declare that they are atheists and carry on living no better lives than their so-called theist counterparts. This conviction primarily comes more from their poor comprehension and lack of patience.

On the other hand, the civic societies are so dominated by market forces that they have put the human spiritual needs on the back seat. No surprises that the so-called post-modern civilisation, which has so beautifully taken care of the material needs of the individuals, has failed miserably to balance it with the psychological and social needs of the citizens. To cut the long argument short, man can never be pleased by undermining his core human value like *Love* and *Truth,* no matter how much he progresses in terms of luxury and material. In these times when the traditional cultures are marred with extremism and the modern civic cultures are plagued with excessive materialism, or should I say extreme hedonism, the world seems to be more in need of the 'moderate' path of Sufis than ever before.

Sufis are known for seeing the Creator in every creation. They are pantheists who perceive God beyond religion and cults and see all scriptures as 'human beautification manuals' and with this orientation, they see entire humanity as one. The following couplet by Hafez, a Persian Sufi, is a testimony to this orientation.

"I am in love with every church
And mosque
And temple
And any kind of shrine
Because I know it is there
That people say the different names
Of the One God."

Sufis have not only played the role of spiritual mentors or cultural reformers but also contributed to society in a thousand other ways as psychologists, chemists, political advisors, adjudicators, poets, writers, and chefs, too. The coffee we drink today is said to have been discovered by the Sufis who lived in the mountains of East Africa and used it as a drink to ward off sleep and focus on late-night meditations.

A few years back, I came across a Sufi story by Ahmed el-Bedavi (d. 1276), an Egyptian Sufi, which in my view is a brilliant example of the Sufi orientation.

"Once upon a time, a man was contemplating how Nature operates, and he discovered, because of his concentration and application, how fire could be made.

This man was named *Nour* (light). He decided to travel from one community to another, showing people his discovery.

Nour passed the secret to many groups of people. Some took advantage of the knowledge, while others drove him away, thinking that he must be dangerous before they had the time to understand how valuable this discovery could be to them. Finally, a tribe before which he demonstrated his discovery became so panic-stricken that they killed him, being convinced that he was a demon.

Centuries passed. The first tribe which had learnt about fire reserved the secret for their priests, who remained in affluence and power while the people froze. The second tribe forgot the art and worshipped the instruments instead. The third worshipped a likeness of Nour himself because it was he who had taught them. The fourth retained the story of the making of fire in their legends; some believed them, some did not. The fifth community really did use fire, and this enabled them to warm themselves, cook their food, and manufacture all kinds of useful articles.

After many more years, a wise man and a small band of his disciples were travelling through the lands of those tribes. The disciples were amazed at the variety of rituals which they encountered. After noticing this, one of the disciples said to their teacher, 'But all these procedures are in fact related to the making of fire, nothing else. We should reform these people!'

The teacher said, 'Very well, then. We shall restart our journey. By the end of it, those who survive will know the real problems and how to approach them.'

When they reached the first tribe, the band was hospitably received. The priests invited the travellers to attend their religious ceremony of the making of fire. When it was over, the master asked, 'Does anyone wish to speak?'

The first disciple said, 'In the cause of truth, I feel myself constrained to say something to these people.'

'If you will do so at your own risk, you may do so,' said the master.

Now the disciple stepped forward in the presence of the tribal chief and his priests, and said, 'I can perform the miracle which you take to be a special manifestation of the deity. If I do so, will you accept that you have been in error for so many years?'

But the priests cried, 'Seize him!' Then the disciple was taken away, never to be seen again.

The travellers went to the next territory where the second tribe was worshipping the instruments of fire-making. Again, a disciple volunteered to try to bring reason to the community. With the permission of the master, he said, 'I beg for your permission to speak to you as reasonable people. You are worshipping the means whereby something may be done, but it's not even the thing itself. Thus, you are suspending the advent of its usefulness. I know the reality that lies at the basis of this ceremony.'

This tribe was composed of more reasonable people. But they said to the disciple, 'You are welcome as a traveller and stranger in our midst. But, as a stranger, foreign to our history and customs, you cannot understand what we are doing. You make a mistake. Perhaps, you are even trying to take away or alter our religion. We, therefore, decline to listen to you.'

The travellers moved on. When they arrived in the land of the third tribe, they found before every dwelling an idol representing Nour, the original fire-maker. The third disciple addressed the chiefs of the tribe, 'This idol represents a man, who represents a capacity, which can be used.'

'This may be so,' interjected one of the Nour-worshippers, 'but the penetration of the real secret is only for the few.'

'It is only for the few who will understand, not for those who refuse to face certain facts,' said the third disciple.

'This is rank heresy, and that, too, from a man who does not even speak our language correctly and is not a priest ordained in our faith,' muttered the priests. And the disciple was unable to make any headway.

The band continued their journey and arrived in the land of the fourth tribe. Now a fourth disciple stepped forward in the assembly of people and said, 'The story of making fire is true, and I know how it may be done.' Confusion broke out within the tribe, which split into various factions. Some said, 'This may be true, and if it is, we want to find out how to make fire.' When the master and his followers examined these people, however, it was found that most of them were anxious to use fire-making for personal advantage and did not realise that it was something for human progress. The many distorted legends had penetrated deep into their minds and those who thought that they might, in fact, represent truth were often the unbalanced ones, who could not have made the fire even if they had been shown how to.

There was another faction, which said, 'Of course, the legends are not true. This man is just trying to fool us to make a place for himself here.'

And a further faction said, 'We prefer the legends as they are the very mortar of our cohesion. If we abandon them and then find that this new interpretation is useless, what will become of our community then?'

So, the party travelled on until they reached the lands of the fifth community, where fire-making was a commonplace and where other preoccupations faced them.

The master said to his disciples, 'You have to learn how to teach, for man does not want to be taught. First of all, you will have to teach people how to learn. And before that, you will have to teach them that there is still something to be learnt. They imagine that they are ready to learn. But they want to learn what they imagine is to be learnt, and not what they first have to learn. When you have learnt all this, then you can devise the way to teach. Knowledge without a special capacity to teach is not the same as knowledge and capacity.'"*

Every book serves a purpose, and if I can define the use of this work, it would be to 'bring you closer to the truth'. Whatever may be your faith, culture, or background, if your human values are alive, this book will not only make perfect sense to you but also help you in bolstering your quest for seeking your perfection . . . your spiritual perfection, if that sounds better.

This is not just another book on Sufism. I promise you, there's enough in here about the Sufi way of life which is a fresh perspective on the subject that takes it beyond the genre of spirituality, psychology, self-help, and science. The book interprets Sufi tools, techniques, and rituals in a way that can make sense in contemporary times.

*Tales of the Dervishes: Idries Shah Foundation

This is an attempt to introduce to you the essence of the philosophical genius of Rumi, unconditional love of Rabia Basri, the heresy of Mansur Hallaj, the logic and inferences of Imam Ghazali, the brilliant storytelling of Farid-ud-Din Attar, the humour of Mulla Nasruddin, the love of the melody of Khwaja Moinuddin Chishti and Amir Khusrow, contemporary westernised touch of Idries Shah, grassroots wisdom of Kabir, *sabr* and *tawakkul* (patience and trust in God's plan) of my great-grand guru Hazrat Waris Ali Shah, my first-hand experience of the spiritual brilliance of my sheikh, Hazrat Roshan Shah Warsi, and last but not the least, the scientific researches that are helping us understand and appreciate our age-old spiritual wisdom in a much better manner.

I have tried to put together all that I have learnt, unlearnt, experienced, stumbled upon, discovered, lost, and rediscovered in the last thirty-five years as a seeker, in a logical and easily relatable language. Hope you will enjoy and benefit from the book as much as I have enjoyed and benefitted from penning it down. Feel free to share your feedback and experiences on the coordinates given on the last page of the book. Wishing you love and light.

Chapter 1

Man's Existential Pain

WHO AM I?

Our biosphere consists of more than 9 million animals and insects and around 250,000 plant species. They appear similar yet distinct, independent yet interdependent. They take birth, grow, thrive, multiply, and ultimately die, very much like humans. Still, none of them grapples with such basic existential questions as 'Who am I?' and 'What is the purpose of my life?' the way we humans do. Maybe, they do suffer from these nagging inklings or maybe not. But there's no certain way of knowing to what extent the animals suffer from this identity crisis as humans do. But as far as we, humans, are concerned, these questions have been the driving force behind all the soul searching done so far by our spiritual exemplars spread across different geographies over ages. Be it St Francis of Assisi, son of a wealthy cloth merchant, or Gautam Buddha, the king who left his luxurious lifestyle to search the higher purpose of life, or St Kabir, the weaver who questioned religious dogmas of his time to reach the truth, or Rumi, who threw away his reputation of a revered scholar after meeting Shams of Tabriz, and the countless others who never made it to records but did their own share of soul searching. History proves that man has had a tough time figuring out his true place under this sun. This identity crisis has been the cause of so many wars and cultural clashes and has also given birth to so many 'isms' over the ages.

Such existential questions trouble us because we are the only species that is bestowed with a very high level of consciousness apart from the ability to feel, sense, memorise, and think. Man, unlike other species, is equipped with the capacity to know where his thinking comes from which is the awareness of consciousness. In spiritual terms, man is born with the capacity to perceive the Creator. This capacity is his unique divine gift. Ironically, this capacity comes with a rider—it is available to him only when he is oriented right, i.e., heart-centred. Inversely, the same gift is reduced to a curse if he is oriented wrong, i.e., ego-centred. In the coming chapters, we will talk about these centres in detail.

Labels That Obscure Our True Nature

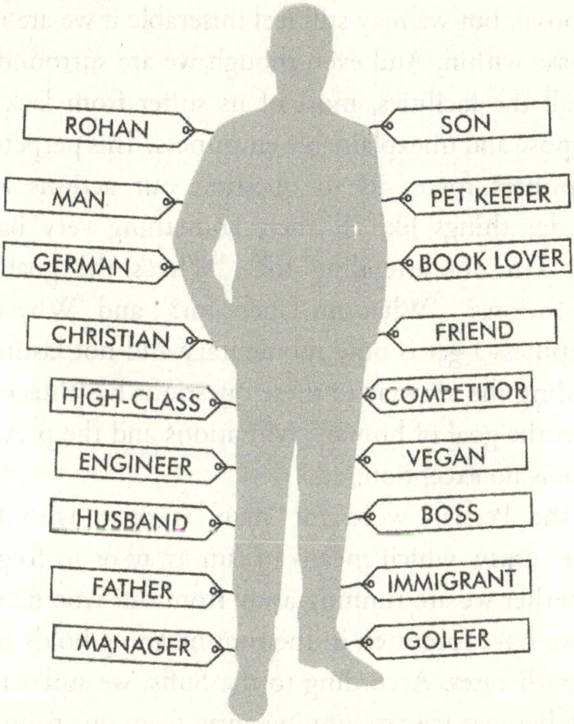

Taking our discussion forward, over these aeons of the evolutionary journey, we humans have evolved to a level where our existence is more consciousness dominated, unlike other creatures, who are primarily bodies being governed by senses and meagre awareness. Consequently, the well-being of humans is more psychological than physical in nature. We may be looking healthy, doing very well outwardly, and enjoying all the luxuries and amenities at our disposal, but we may still feel miserable if we are not at ease within. And even though we are surrounded by all the facilities, most of us suffer from lack of purpose and unexplainable emptiness. This perpetual emptiness forces us to question our actions and ponder things like 'Is there something very basic that I'm not attending to?', 'What's the goal of my actions?', 'What am I here for?', and 'Why the happiness I get is only momentary and not lasting?' Finding the answers to these questions has thus ever been the goal of human civilisations and the present time is no exception.

The Persian word for 'man' is *insan* with the root *nisyan,* which means to run away or to forget. Whether we are running away from our true nature or we have forgotten it, the root meaning holds true in both cases. According to the Sufis, we suffer this way because we are running away from our primary nature—Love. But what is this love? And how is it different from the love we all know. Before we move further, let me share a hint dropped by Rumi, the great Sufi poet: "Wherever you are, whatever you do, be in love." Here, Rumi is advising us to be always aware of our essential nature and not disown it in any situation.

Apart from saints, scientists and all religions have tried to interpret and explain our primary nature in their own unique ways. Let us take up their explanations one by one.

Science

The biosphere has billions of animal and plant. More and more are added periodically, whereas a certain number die out as well. The surviving species give birth to young ones and, as they say, "Life goes on." In this process, the next generation of every species also evolves incrementally to adapt to ever-changing conditions. Some otherwise terrestrial, learn to climb trees, some develop special skins, larger brains, more agile bodies, etc. All these adaptations help them survive and evolve into fitter species than their ancestors.

Man has also been part of this so-called open world for most of his evolutionary journey. He was not as strong as a lion, as big as an elephant, or as fast as a cheetah, but in this struggle for survival vis-à-vis other species, nature gifted him with brain development and better mental capacity. This gave humans a tremendous advantage on their evolutionary journey. Now, the man wasn't just endowed with instincts, memories, and sense organs like most other fellow animals, but something unique also got added to his neurology: consciousness of consciousness (the ability to perceive intent, thoughts, emotions, behaviour, actions, etc.). This is also described as 'awareness' or 'mindfulness' in modern-day language.

What Is Consciousness?

Every material that exists, living or dead, is conscious on some level. Be it atom that behaves only in a certain manner, a chemical reaction that follows a set pattern, a piece of wood with unique properties, or an animal who displays a typical behaviour . . . all are conscious. Still, comparatively speaking, a plant is more conscious than dead wood, an animal is more conscious than a plant, and man is the most conscious of the lot. Coming back to awareness, it may be defined as an overarching sensor of our five senses, memories, beliefs, thoughts, feelings, and, of course, the body and its consciousness or overall state. While other animals also employ their mental faculties in varying degrees, but they are more or less slaves of their senses and innate tendencies and thus, are not aware of their actions. On the other hand, man, if aware of his state, can master his senses, tendencies, and thoughts, and hence, the resulting actions as well. This is what is called as 'will' which is the mastery over the choice of our actions. This awareness is the finest element of the human make-up, but it is also easiest to lose. Even the slightest mental disturbance can rob us of this miraculous capacity and send us tumbling to a lower level of consciousness. This causes us to fall back on established patterns that have worked in the past (beliefs) rather than tackling every situation from a fresh and unique perspective, and in doing so, we start reacting instead of responding. We look around for inspiration, copy others, and start behaving like sheep. Further add memories, conditioning, prejudices, and fears to this situation and we have a very unhealthy psychological state. Unfortunately, this is the state most humans exist in these days and operate from.

Have you heard of stress among wild animals? Have you heard of a lion hiring a contract killer lion to kill a rival in yonder forest, just because he hates him? Or have you heard of an animal committing suicide? "Of course not!" you will say.

Coming back to our discussion, when we are not aware of our state and actions, we might behave worse than animals by not allowing our superior mental capacity free play. In this situation, our choices of action become faulty and we start living an unhealthy lifestyle and such a way of life is not good for us, our family, and humanity at large. Scientists have concluded that humans don't have a fixed nature or behaviour. Rather, their behaviour is floating somewhere between two extremes of innumerable action choices available to them in any given situation. They can be honest at one time and dishonest at another, reasonable in some situations and unreasonable in others. In a nutshell, we humans can choose what we want to 'be' in a given situation. That's why we are called 'human be-ings'.

PLUTCHIK'S WHEEL

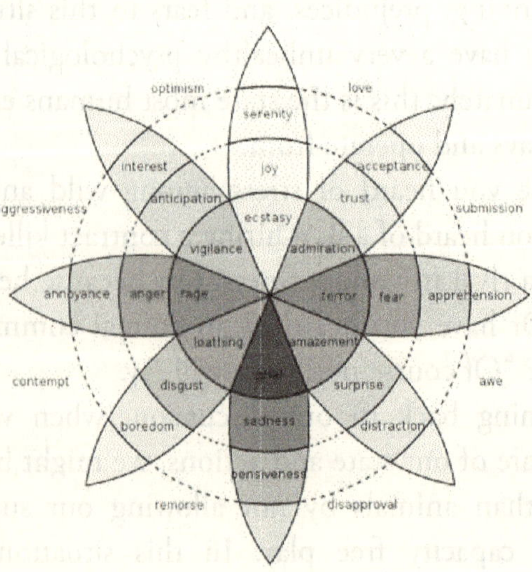

There is no given way in which a human will respond to a situation unlike, say, a dog, a cat, or a mouse. It is interesting to note, the quality of our action depends solely on how aware we are at a given point of time. It is this sensitivity to our state that forces us to question our actions and existence in general. It is this quest for one's best state or fulfilment that has caused so many seekers to leave their homes for the mountains or other places of seclusion. From science, let's move on to explanations offered by religion.

Religion

Before I touch upon this, let me sensitise the reader about the orientation of my explanation. The core context of this explanation is that 'God is one' and all the different religions and organised belief systems are different paths to connect us to the same truth. All religions employ symbolism and metaphors to denote the phenomena otherwise not visible to the naked eye or detected by the senses. These phenomena need the finer faculties like the vagus nerve or extra sensory perceptions for them to be detected.

According to Hindu tradition, when a child is born (after the umbilical cord is snapped), he is thrown into the world of duality which is so drastically different from the state of non-duality and perfect bliss he experienced in his mothers' womb, where he never felt hunger pangs, thirst, or the need to breathe. After birth, he misses this non-dual state and tries to recall it. This is the reason we cry out the question, *"Ko hamm? Ko hamm?"* (Who am I? Who am I?). This is the same existential question we talked about earlier. To help man deal with this identity crisis, since the beginning of time, prophets, avatars, messengers of God, and saints have been appearing in different cultures to guide their communities on to the right path—the path which brings them closer to their true nature. In other words, to help them align with the supreme consciousness or God. According to most religions, once perfectly aligned with the supreme consciousness, our actions bring better results which ultimately ensures us a place in heaven or causes us to burn in hell, if we deviate from it.

Man, according to religion, suffers when he doesn't see himself as one with the whole and starts treating himself as a separate entity ('I' consciousness). By doing so, he gets psychologically cut off from God or the supreme consciousness that guides him to live in harmony with the rest of the biosphere/universe. Both the Hindu concept of *advait* and that of *tauhid* in Islam refer to this idea of non-duality or oneness. Basically, their purpose is to nudge the man towards a state where he may realise his true place under the sun; a state in which he is able to do justice to his brilliant potential.

Spirituality

Ever since man appeared on the face of the earth, spiritual practices all over the world, whether associated with popular religions or independent of them, have helped man connect to his higher potential using different meditative practices and rituals.

The majority of the modalities proclaim that God lives in the heart of man—a symbolic heart located on the left side of the chest. According to spiritual masters, till the man is soul-centred or heart-centred, he is in perfect alignment with the supreme consciousness or God. But if he becomes body-centric or egocentric, his connection with the supreme consciousness gets snapped and, as a result, he loses his perfection which causes him immense psychological pain and suffering. Missing it badly, he tries to regain this lost state by searching for solace among material objects in the outside world and doing things that give him sensual gratification, but never succeeds. Kabir, the famous 15th-century Sufi of Banaras, has beautifully put this in his following verse:

"Kasturi kundali base mrig dhoondhe van mahi,
yun hi ghat-ghat ram hain, duniya jane nahin."

(Musk lies in the navel of the musk deer and he
runs around in the forest chasing its smell.)

In the same manner, there is God in every heart and the world doesn't know.

The Sufis have equated man's quest for the lost perfection with that of a lover seeking his beloved. Here, the beloved is *guru* or *sheikh,* and, at a later stage, the God. Popular Sufi literature like the love poems of Rumi, folk love stories like 'Laila Majnu' and 'Heer Ranjha', and the Persian Sufi masterpiece, *The Conference of the Birds*, by Farid-ud-Din Attar are all beautiful allegories of this striving to meet the beloved, which ends up in the lover finding the perfection within.

Many mystical schools of the East, on the other hand, help individuals move to a higher consciousness by channelising energies through *kundalini* awakening and *chakra* unblocking. Here, the topmost chakra, the crown chakra, represents *Brahm*, the highest level of consciousness humans can experience. Whatever may be the path one chooses to follow, the bottom line for all spiritual modalities remain the same and that is to help the seeker achieve wholeness, completeness . . . human perfection.

What is the higher human potential?

"You were born with wings, why prefer to crawl through life."

— Rumi

The French philosopher and Jesuit priest, Pierre Teilhard de Chardin, has remarked, "We are not physical beings having a spiritual experience. We are spiritual beings having a physical experience."

This implies that human existence is spirit or psyche dominated rather than physiology dominated, as it is generally believed. Therefore, our well-being is affected and determined more by what we think and feel than by what we eat or possess. In other words, our happiness depends more on our mental state than on our physical or material assets.

Nearly all the spiritual paths agree that man is a microcosm, an ocean in a drop. That is, the small entity in the macrocosm that is man, encapsulates in his consciousness the entire cosmos itself. Yes, we are simply infinite in terms of potential as most motivational speakers push us to believe, but we are limited as physical bodies. How much of this potential is available to us at any given point of time depends on our level of consciousness. In short, raising our level of consciousness and consolidating awareness of states is the ultimate purpose of all spiritual practices, including Sufism. How they bring this about is the subject of the upcoming chapters.

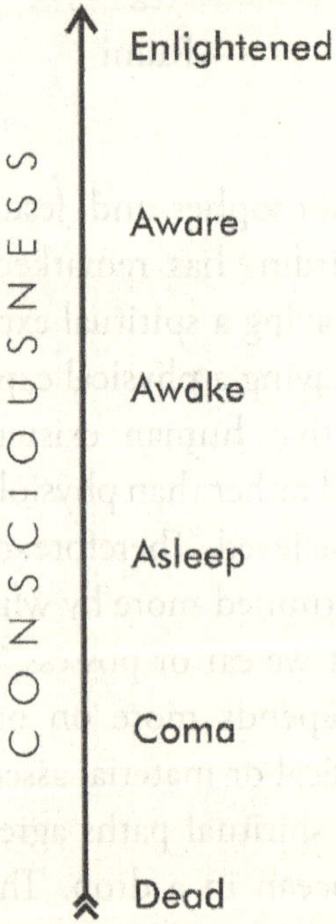

To understand the correlation between our consciousness and our ability to see and observe things in a given situation, let's spend some time understanding Aristotle's cause model.

Aristotle's doctrine of the four causes

(Four-Levels of observation)

1. The Formal Cause

This refers to what gives matter its form.
Here, the TV with screen, speaker and channel knob.

2. The Material Cause

This is the substance that something is made of.
For example, a TV is made of glass and metal and plastic.

3. The Final Cause

This cause is the reason why something is the way it is.
The Final Cause is the reason why a thing exists in the first place, its function.

4. The Efficient Cause

This refers to the creator behind the creation.
For example, a TV exists because someone had the idea to build one and put all the parts together to make it work.

An observer who is at the lowest level of consciousness will be able to see only the Formal Cause or level 1 (form and shape of creation) of life and situations which is devoid of finer reflective capacity and sensibilities. He only believes in what he can see with his eyes. For such people, 'seeing is believing'. Next comes the Material Cause or level 2 (composition of the creation) when the observer can not only just perceive something but reflect upon it and understand what it is made of. At the level of the Final Cause or level 3 (the reason behind creation), the observer can see the intent behind the creation of something. Once he manages to see up to level 3, the Efficient Cause or level 4 (the Creator) is revealed to him. Or we could say, at this level, his understanding of the creation is in alignment with that of the Creator, as he gets the clarity about the purpose behind the creation as intended by the Creator. In spiritual terms, it is said that the 'observer becomes one with the observed' at this level. No wonder God is said to have bestowed 'light' on man in most cultures . . . a light that helps him see the truth through illusions. This ability to see through the causes is true not only of physical objects but psychological states, feelings, and thoughts, too.

Let us understand this through an everyday life analogy. Say, you lose your temper over some incident. If you are at a very low level of consciousness, you may not detect anything about this anger-trigger and be consumed by it, letting it do damage at the emotional and psychological levels. It may force you to react in a destructive manner, only to repent later. Not only this, but you may also carry the hangover of this unpleasant incident to the rest of the day and even much later. Add a few more similar reactions to more such triggers in different incidents, and it adds up to form your behaviour pattern. This is the case for many of our friends who are branded short-tempered by their peer group. Unfortunately, this is happening every day to many of us and we are not conscious enough even to take note of it.

As your consciousness improves, you get better equipped to salvage yourself. Here's how it dovetails with the Aristotelian cause model. At level 1, you can see the anger (who is angry) and at level 2, you can observe the shortening of breath, adrenaline rush, sweat on the forehead, shivering hands, and increased blood pressure (what is happening to you). If you are more conscious to be on level 3, you can see the reason behind this reaction (the 'why' of the anger). And on level 4, the Creator of this reaction, 'the source' creating the anger is revealed to you (Please refer to 'Intent' in the Principles and Doctrines section). More often than not, the source of the trigger is your ego. At this level of awareness, you will be able to see the truth of the situation and choose the best response from all the response options available to you which are beyond your conditioning driven automated reactions.

This discretionary capacity of choosing a response outside of your belief system is called emotional intelligence in modern-day language. All in all, a higher version of the individual is revealed as his level of consciousness keeps improving.

This capacity is very beautifully explained by Ali-Ibn Talib in the following comment:

"God, the Exalted, gave angels intellect without desires, He gave animals desires without

intellect, and He gave both to the sons of Adam. So a man whose intellect prevails over his desires is better than angels, whilst a man whose desire prevails over his intellect is worse than animals."

To conclude, the highest human potential is the highest level of consciousness which can cut through the layers of beliefs and illusions and arrive at the truth (levels 3 and 4 of Aristotle's model) in everything he feels, experiences, and sees.

Does spirituality have any place in modern life?

Look around yourself and at yourself. Don't you find most of us edgy, over-entertained, stressed, and in a hurry these days? We start our day weighed down by the stress of the previous day. We eat faster than we should and fail to register the taste when we are eating. The fast-food manufacturers are having a tough time preparing even faster food to cater to our ever-increasing speed eating preferences. Thanks to the electronic gadgets at our disposal, the social media is constantly pulling our attention and because of which our focus is getting fragmented and our awareness is suffering immensely. We are losing the art of planning and are being dominated by an ever-agitated mind that works in a random manner. We forget our promises and have to work extra hard to honour our commitments. We are more often than not late for our meetings. We react to situations instead of responding. In Steven Covey's language, we are so busy attending to the 'urgent' that we have no time for the 'important'. We wear careworn looks or frowns on our faces rather than smiles. We are eating unhealthy and filling up our systems with refined sugars, booze, and caffeine to keep ourselves going. Our craving for high-decibel emotional charges is rising at an alarming rate. Stand-up comedians have to work extra hard to make us laugh. Our new generations are even more self-centred and self-obsessed than the previous ones. We are exposed to more negative and fear-inducing news 24x7 or highly dramatic reality shows. We are spending a good percentage of our monthly earnings on health check-ups. And last but not the least, we are in danger of being swept away by the tsunami of content. This deluge of content is seeking to replace real experience with virtual experience in almost every walk of life. It won't be an exaggeration to say that modern society is getting 'virtual' at the cost of the 'real'.

All these disturbances and soft agitations are unprecedented challenges to our consciousness and they very subtly drag it down to a level where our inherent awareness or spiritual sharpness gets blunted and we are left with a capacity which, at best, can only help us live a gross (egocentric) life. Thus, when we live a life dominated by belief patterns and conditioning, we fail to access our finer intuitive faculties that have the potential to put us in touch with the reality, the truth.

But why does this happen in the first place and what are the causes behind it? In my opinion, we are losing touch with our higher consciousness due to the constant chatter and clamour agitating our mental, physical, and social world round the clock. This forces us to take faulty decisions and make unhealthy lifestyle choices. A smartphone bereft of all its high-end features, behaving like a basic cell phone, may be an apt, if ironical, parallel. The fact is that wherever they may be coming from and whatever may be the reasons or excuses we tender for allowing these to mould our lives, the characteristics of the modern age that I have spelt out are taking their toll on our health, both physical and mental, and adversely affecting our relationships, productivity, spirituality, and life in general.

In these trying, nerve-wracking times, going back to our primordial nature, which is 'love' is a luxury not many of us can afford. Hence, we look around for quick-fix pain relievers. Because we cannot afford a cure, we seem satisfied with solutions that can partly or momentarily alleviate our symptoms and mental pain. This way we seek to fulfil our spiritual longing with distractions like sports, entertainment, liquor, drugs, fashion, and parties, and try to be true to the outside world while betraying our inner selves. Even when we claim to be making efforts to seek our spiritual side, most of us fall victim to emotionality, ritualism, culturalism, superstition, astrology, occult practices, and energy healing. Consequently, we waste a lot of precious time trying to fit these square bolts in the round holes of our spiritual need. I often hear in spiritual circles that people are losing interest in exploring their higher consciousness. Well, they are, in fact, losing their spiritual capacity and not just interest.

The world is full of knowledge about human development though we may not be able to apply them due to many reasons cited above. Every culture, society, and civilisation has left legacies in science, craft, governance, literature, and spirituality. Sufism is one such legacy for humanity. Its tools techniques and practices are so universal that it can make sense to people of any culture, creed, or orientation provided they approach it from their essential nature of love. Most of the seekers who are interested in Sufism pick their *sheikhs* (guides) among the organised schools of thought called orders or *tariqas.* These orders have some unique rituals and practices that are based on their cultures and situations. The Sufi order that has become popular over these years and still attracts hordes of new seekers is the Mevlevi order, named after Mevlana Jalal ad-Din Muhammad Rumi. This is the most popular order in the West. Four large tariqas common in South Asia are: the Naqshbandi (named after Baha-ud-Din Naqshband Bukhari), the Qadiria (named after Abdul Qadir Gilani), the Chishtia (named after Khwaja Moinuddin

Chishti), and the Suhrawardia (named after Shahab al-Din Suhrawardi). Popular tariqas in Africa include Muridiyya and Tijaniyya. There are other sub-orders like Qalandariyya that have roots in Malamatiyya (with Buddhism and Hinduism influence) and Ashrafia which is the sub-branch of Chishti spiritual lineage. This book is not sticking to the modus operandi of any particular school of thought but tries to highlight the universal Sufi values that go not just beyond these orders but religion, too.

Just for the technical reasons, I would like to sensitise the reader that the term 'Sufi' stands for the final refined product of this journey of self-perfection. A seeker is best described as a dervish. I have used the word 'Sufi' as a generic term just for the sake of simplicity. On this note, let me introduce you to the beautiful path of the Sufis with a hope that you will be able to join a few dots on your own to figure a way out of this messy psychological situation and find your way back home.

Chapter 2

Welcome to Sufism!

"The Man of God is made wise by the Truth.
The man of God is not learned from the book."
— Rumi

There has been a recent revival of interest in Sufis and Sufi mysticism. Over the centuries, they have always attracted followers and common people. Almost all serious spiritual seekers, no matter which philosophy they practice, seem to be intrigued by these enigmatic characters who represent love, freedom, and pantheism—the virtues all of us crave even more in these stressful and divisive times, when the human society is faced with unprecedented challenges from the segregating forces of caste, class, religion, state, etc.

Sufis are popularly designated as Muslim mystics, wandering dervishes, or *faquirs*, gurus, sheikhs, or peers (old man) in different parts of the world, but are also known by the qualities they possess, for example, *ahl-e-qalb* (people of the heart) and *ahl-e-haqq* (people of truth). Some claim that they are found in one form or the other in all major world religions, be it Islam, Christianity, Hinduism, Judaism, and even in the native faiths. Others argue that as the

Sufis perceive all religions to be one and the same, they shouldn't be bracketed in any one religion. On one hand, the orthodox refuse to own them for their queer behaviour and non-conformist attitude and on the other, people from almost every religion respect them for their sincere behaviour and practice of the highest human values of truth and love. Sufis, or perhaps we should say Sufi-like people, in all ages and parts of the world, have been guiding people to find their true potential whether collectively or as select disciples. Sometimes, their efforts and wisdom have been welcomed and appreciated and at other times, have been received with indifference or even opposed by orthodox regimes.

Those who have travelled the world would vouch that they have encountered Sufis almost everywhere, be it Morocco or Malaysia, South Africa or Serbia, Bangladesh or Bangalore, Chennai or Constantinople. You may spot them wearing yellow or white robes in India, black ones in Baghdad, green ones in Ethiopia, or even patched gowns in some other part of the world. In some cultures, they sing praises of God and, in others, they chant and howl, dance and whirl, hop and sway. They do breathing exercises in some social milieus, while meditate in others. They can be found following orthodox rituals in one region while behaving very unconventionally in yet another part of the globe.

They have been known to be hated by some kings and treated like mentors by others. Some of them wrote books, while some didn't. Some married and a good few didn't. There have been Sufi saints with a huge following and some whom people have despised and shunned. Some, like Imam Ghazali, were great orthodox scholars of their time, while some, like Kabir, were content imparting spiritual wisdom through hymns while weaving clothes for a living. A few, like Baba Nanak, became the founders of a new religion, while some, like Baba Bulleh Shah, chose to live a humble life, renouncing the legacy of a respectable lineage. Some ran hermitages (*khankahs*) where hundreds of initiates benefited from their teachings by following prescribed rituals, while some preferred to live a secluded life, cut-off from the hustle and bustle of the society. A good number went about living normal lives with a slightly unorthodox attitude which could be detected only on close observation. There have been a few Sufis who were surrounded by wealth as kings, but the majority preferred living austere lives, giving away all that they possessed in the service of humanity. There have been Sufis who preached, while many maintained a distance from people and happily lived self-contained lives. (For the information of the reader, a preacher is not considered as the highest station among Sufis).

If such is the outward diversity of the Sufis, how does one spot a true one? As I have already mentioned, a Sufi may very well be living a normal life among all of us and without us knowing about it. He may be your lawyer, neighbour, somebody's driver, gardener, a sales executive, a caring mother, a surgeon, or a barber. They may look like ordinary people, but inwardly, they enjoy a state (*hal*) that many saints aspire to achieve. This is what Rumi says about them:

"Fools buy false coins because they are like true.
If in the world no genuine minted coins were current, how would forgers pass the false?
Falsehood was nothing unless the truth were there, to make it specious.
'Tis the love of right that lures men to wrong.
Let poison but be mixed with sugar, they will cram it into their mouths.
Oh, cry not that all creeds are vain!
Some scent of truth they have, else they would not beguile.
Say not, 'How utterly fantastical!'
No fancy in the world is all untrue.

Amongst the crowd of dervishes hides one,
One true faqir. Search well and thou wilt
find!"
— *The Mystics of Islam*, R.A. Nicholson

Here's an attempt to demystify this mystery for the reader. There are three essential constituents to a Sufi's make-up and the extent to which he has each of them collectively adds up to determine his rank. These three constituents are:

a) Knowledge
b) State
c) Service

A Sufi has knowledge about himself and his ego derived from personal experience. It isn't merely bookish learning or second-hand knowledge but knowledge that is also honed and validated through the first-hand experience. Because he believes in experiencing God, this experience leaves him in a certain state that he operates from. His actions flow out from his state (being) and aren't just rituals approved by his culture. So much so that at times he may appear at odds vis-à-vis the cultural norms to be true to his state. Many Sufis like Mansoor Hallaj and Sarmad (the martyr) are examples of this. Stories of Mulla Nasruddin or Bahlol Dana (the wise fool of

Baghdad) are again examples of a Sufi who is wise sometimes and appears a fool at other times. It is a pity that most of us draw our conclusions about these saintly figures by their outward appearance (form and looks) without digging deeper to understand their behaviour and weighing them on any of the three parameters I mentioned earlier. In fact, what we manage to perceive of a Sufi is only what we are capable of perceiving, which actually holds true for everything that we see. As it has famously been said, "To understand a Sufi, you have to be half Sufi." The following story highlights the role of a Sufi in society.

"Once upon a time, a wealthy man passed through a town. He stopped his caravan outside an inn and called out to four people. They ran towards him and presenting them with a gold coin, he instructed: 'This money is to be shared amongst you.' Saying this, he then went on his way.

The first man was a Persian and said: 'With this money, I will buy some *angur*!' The second was an Arab and he said, 'No, you can't because I want to buy *inab*!' The third, a Turk, said: 'I don't want *inab*, I want *uzum*!' The fourth was a Greek and he said: 'I don't want what any of you want. I want to buy *stafil*!' Since they did not know each other's language, the four started to fight. They imagined that each wanted to use the coin to buy a different fruit. What they didn't know is that all of them were actually talking about the same fruit and hence, their differences were meaningless. They had information, but no knowledge. Luckily, a wise man was going to the inn. He paused to see what the commotion was about and asked them, 'What is the problem here?' They narrated the entire story and he said, 'Ah! I can fulfil the wishes of all of you with one and the same gold coin, if you put your trust in me. They agreed. He went to a nearby fruit seller and got a bagful of grapes. Looking at the grapes, all of them shouted with delight: 'Ahha . . . *angur*!', '*Inab*!', 'My *uzum*!' and 'Here are my *stafil*!' respectively."

Only a person of great wisdom would know that each of them wanted the same thing—grapes. So is the case with many cultures, ideas, and religions that have many things in common, but they are not aware of it.

In the above story, the travellers are ordinary religious people and the wise man who understands their languages is a Sufi. I would like to conclude this section with the following lines:

"In constant communion with the Beloved within,
a stranger to the world.
Those endowed with such beauty are rare indeed in this world."

— Anonymous

ANOTHER NAME FOR THE SAME

Sufis believe that man, first and foremost, is a being . . . a state (*hal*). This state that an individual enjoys is an outcome of the level of his awareness (*muqam*) which is a result of the elevation of consciousness. The more he is able to observe/perceive phenomena, the higher his state of being. And a higher state brings him closer to his true nature which is love. At the peak of this level, he sees everything in the universe as one and an interconnected whole including himself. So, his 'loving' state is a result of the orientation of his *tauhid* or *advait*. The Sufi initiate strives to achieve this state through *tazkiya* (purification), self-observation, meditative exercises, and emulating the *sheikh*.

Unlike many other spiritual modalities, it is the inner *batin* or state of the *sheikh* that disciples and followers respect and try to emulate. They are watchful towards not getting caught up with his outward appearance, persona, or *zahir* (image).

Let me explain how Sufism as a modality is different from or similar to other spiritual streams with the help of the following diagram. Putting it simplistically, we can say that human thoughts give way to emotions and emotions, whether regulated or unregulated by the intellect, drive our action or behaviour.

Most spiritual practices act exclusively on one level or on a combination of these levels through their rituals and transformation techniques to bring about the aspirational shift in the state of the practitioner. Chakra unblocking, kundalini awakening, yoga postures, inspirational stories, mantra chants, meditation techniques, energy healing, and even not so dramatic looking things like feeding the birds and helping the poor are all ultimately aimed at altering unhealthy thought patterns and channelising and shifting the energies, which results in ensuring a balanced and healthy life to the practitioner.

Apart from the linear intervention models, there are practices that go a little deeper and address things from the holistic level of awareness or being from where intent, thought, emotions, actions, behaviours, memories, beliefs, conditioning, assumptions, and patterns can be collectively influenced and thus altered. Sufism believes in this kind of holistic approach and is open to any and every tool of transformation necessary to bring about a shift in the orientation and ultimately, the behaviour of the seeker. Thus, the end goal of such intervention becomes elevation of the state of being, and, once that is achieved, the behaviours and actions become secondary. In other words, you just take care of your being and the doing will be taken care of by the supreme consciousness, as it is the best judge of actions needed in a given situation. This is the formula followed by the Sufis.

As far as helping others move up the ladder of states is concerned, the *sheikh* (mentor) himself must have experienced and stabilised himself in the state he's trying to induce in his disciple or he will falter and the intervention could even be counterproductive for the pupil. It will be apt to mention here that, unlike many other popular modalities, Sufism is a prescription drug and not an over-the-counter one. So, a Sufi *sheikh* is, in medical terms, someone with diagnostic capacity, prescription ability, and pharmacotherapeutic skill rolled into one. He is somebody who not only knows the way but has also travelled down the path personally before playing guide. Hence, he not only has knowledge of the map, but, having traversed the path himself, is aware of the pitfalls, speed breakers, necessary requirements of travel along with the physical capacity required for travel. For the sheikh, as noted earlier, actions are secondary while that which gives birth to the actions, the intent, is of primary importance. It is the intent that determines whether an action will bring about positive spiritual growth or have a negative impact on the novice.

Allow me to share an analogy to make you better understand the specificity of the Sufi path. It is in fashion to treat meditation and other spiritual exercises like multivitamin tablets—something that's universally beneficial, irrespective of the condition of the patient. But the rituals and practices of Sufis are like targeted antibiotics and they should be prescribed and administered with care and responsibility or they may do more damage than good. Many of the so-called Sufi masters have been found violating this rule for the sake of getting popularity and acceptance, but this is an altogether different subject of discussion.

Sufi beliefs and orientation

"The Sufis believe that they can experience something more complete."

— Idries Shah

Sufism is based on the premise that man while operating from his lower self which is dominated by material aspirations, is living a limited life and hence, can never feel fulfilled. This egocentric or 'I' oriented life needs to be challenged to reach a more evolved soul-centric or heart-centric state where lies the true human potential which has the capacity to fetch that elusive peace, joy, love, and fulfilment that all of us crave for. Another interesting thing to note here is the fact that the soul-centre that Sufis refer to is our primordial nature and not a learnt behaviour or an acquired value. Therefore, all that the seeker is supposed to do is remove the dust from the mirror of the soul and enjoy its shine. There is no need for any additional plating or painting. Yes, for those obsessed with doing, removing the dust itself is an enormous task, as we shall see in the pages to come.

According to the Sufis, the spiritual capacity of the seeker depends on how aware he is in the moment and how effectively he frees himself from the clutches of beliefs, conditioning, imaginations, assumptions, labels, indoctrinations, fears, etc. This goes on to determine how clearly he will manage to see the *haq* (truth), which ultimately determines the efficacy of his actions in the given moment. There's a popular saying by prophet Muhammad (PBUH), *"Man arfa nafsuhu, faqad arfa rabbuhu"* (One who knows the self [ego, I], knows the Lord). This idea is the core belief of Sufis of all schools across the world, whether they spell it in these words or not. It is this knowledge that is of paramount importance for humans, as only awareness of the 'I' can help them guard their 'being'. To my understanding, this knowledge, if applied properly, helps us achieve what is today called by names like higher consciousness, awareness, mindfulness, etc.

According to Sufis, good and bad, right and wrong are not absolute. They are relative in nature. What is good in one situation may prove bad in others. For example, wearing a fur coat on a sunny afternoon is a good thing in Siberia but a bad thing in the Sahara. So, whether a behaviour is right or wrong is best decided only by its context. But if we are not conscious of our own discretionary capacity, we will be left to act out of our conditioning whatever the place, time, or requirement, and because of it, we might miss seeing life beyond it.

Further, a so-called good thing may become bad if we take it to the extreme. Overeating is the first example that comes to my mind. The prefix 'over' to any good action and watch it go from good to bad in almost all situations. Therefore, moderation and being true to the situation are handy keywords for a Sufi seeker.

As discussed earlier, human beings don't have a fixed nature and hence, their behaviour can be altered, conditioned, or indoctrinated with the continuous hammering of certain types of messages and by stoking base aspirations and showcasing them as desired values and yardsticks of social acceptability. Such conditioned individuals lose touch with their primary nature and start living like slaves of their conditioning and die justifying the 'I' (fake image of self that they believe to be true). Pampering and boosting their ego further becomes the aspiration and goal of their lives. And at a lower level of consciousness, as one has access to sensual capacity only, they go on pleasing their senses by indulging in music, food, sex, high emotional charges, entertainment, etc., further consolidating 'I', the image they have of themselves and the good life, while totally ignoring the intuitive capacity that can help them connect to who they really are. As these sensual pleasures have no long-lasting fulfilment to offer, this seeking of sensual pleasure never ends, even when the senses grow weak with age.

On the other hand, when a man centres himself on *qalb* (the heart), he sees himself and consequently, the world around him, in a better light. While recognising and fulfilling his sensual and bodily needs, he is not consumed by them as in the case of a common man. The realised man can clearly see his own conditioning, beliefs, assumptions, and prejudices and by the virtue of this, he gets liberated from their clutches or limitations. He sees the range of options available to him and acts as the master of these options, in stark contrast to the few automated conditioned responses he was otherwise accustomed to. After the individual is able to see his 'I' and its limitations, he surrenders his will (desires or what a conditioned mind wants to do) to the truth of the moment and lives free and empowered. After becoming aware of his ego-centre (fear mode), his centre automatically shifts to soul/heart . . . his essential nature, i.e., love, compassion, and service.

For a Sufi, acts of service to humanity are not done for social applause (as the common man who tries to copy their rituals and good acts believes); they are born out of his centring himself on his essential nature or love state, which can flower only after decimating one's ego or *nafs* (fake self-image). This is illustrated in the following story by al-Ghazali:

"One day, a dervish (spiritual man) came to the teacher Bayazid and said, 'I have fasted and prayed for thirty years and have found none of the spiritual joy of which you speak.'

'Even if you fasted and prayed for three hundred years, you would never find it,' answered the sage.

'Why is that?' asked the man.

'Your ego is acting as a veil between you and God.'

'Tell me the cure.'

'It is a cure you cannot carry out,' said Bayazid.

Those around him pressed him to reveal it. After a time he spoke, 'Go to the nearest barbershop and have your head shaved. Strip yourself of your saintly robe, just retaining your loincloth. Take a nosebag full of walnuts, hang it around your neck. Go into the market and cry out: "Anybody who gives me a slap on the neck shall have a walnut." Then proceed to the law courts and the crossroads near your house and do the same thing.'

'I can't do that,' said the man. 'Suggest some other remedy.'

'This is the indispensable preliminary to the cure,' answered Bayazid. 'But as I told you, you are incurable.'"

The Principles and Doctrines

Almost every religion teaches that God which lives in every temple, church, or mosque can also be found in a pure heart. This is the starting point of Sufi orientation. The next step is of course to find ways of establishing a connection with Him who is within all of us, yet with whom we remain out of touch. Doing away with the veils that obscure Him from our view and knowing His likes and dislikes become the primary challenges for a Sufi seeker.

A Sufi claims himself to be a lover of God. And, as one is expected to leave no stone unturned to please the beloved, a Sufi, after learning the likes and dislikes of the beloved does the same. In this process, he forsakes all of his bad habits, actions, and thoughts that might vex the beloved and, in due course, his old habits get replaced with new ones that are desirable to the beloved. Every ritual, exercise, or endeavour of a Sufi is aimed at pleasing the beloved and nothing else. Allow me to quote two prominent Sufi poets to illustrate this:

"Parh parh ilm kitaabaan da tu naam rakh leya qaazi
Hath vich parh ke talvaaraan tu naam rakh leya ghaazi
Makke Madinay ghoom aya tu naam rakh leya haaji
Bullah tu ki haasil kita je yaar na rakhya raazi!"

— Bulleh Shah

(Learning through the knowledge of books you call yourself a scholar.
Grasping the sword in your hand you call yourself a warrior of the lord.
Having visited Mecca and Medina you call yourself a pilgrim.
Bullah, what have you accomplished if you have not remained true to your friend!)

***

"In your light, I learn how to love. In your beauty, how to make poems. You dance inside my chest where no one sees you, but sometimes I do, and that sight becomes this art."

— Rumi

This attitude may be equated with the dropping of one's will and surrendering to the divine will. In doing so, the lover experiences the beautiful flow of perfection that he would have otherwise never felt in the past. And once hooked to it, he strives to never lose it. Great Sufi poet, Amir Khusrow, has this to say about it:

> *"Ye kis muqam pe laya junoon khuda jaane,*
> *sambhal-sambhal ke kadam rakh rahen hain*
> *deewane."*
> (Only God knows the place where passion
> has brought them. The madmen are taking
> every step with utter caution.)

Nature of Man

Sufis believe man is a unique creation whose nature is not fixed but floating. If such is the case, then who is responsible for this floating nature? Today, we use many terms like consciousness, awareness, emotional intelligence, extrasensory perception (ESP), etc., to explain this complex capacity. But thousands of years ago, Sufis cited the example of a ride and the rider to explain the unique nature of humans for the understanding of the then common man. Here the ride refers to the 'body' and rider is used to refer to the 'awareness'.

To make it more contemporary, let us say there is a car that is driven by two different drivers. One driver (soul) is a well-trained and qualified but is a simpleton while the other driver (ego) is only half qualified but very high-headed. Our body is the car that is assigned these two drivers at the time of our birth. If we look back at the journey of our life thus far, all the times when we have been in the flow of things, enjoying a smooth ride, we were being driven by the better driver (soul). On the contrary, whenever we have been angry, jealous, and stressed, it has led to the car going about hitting other vehicles, jumping over speed breakers, ramming into the poles, and eventually, suffering a lot of bruises and dents. As a vehicle, such experiences might have only left us with bad memories. We can easily conclude that it was the bad driver (ego) who was in the driving seat in those moments. If it is so, who decides which driver is to drive the car at any given point of time? Well, that's the role of awareness. The higher our level of awareness, the greater our control over deciding who will drive the car at any point in time. The bad driver (ego), being high headed and stubborn, will invariably jump into the driving seat the moment the radar of awareness becomes a little unwatchful or weak. When awareness is alert, it's the better driver (soul) who gets the chance to drive the car. In the long run, it is advisable for the car to be driven by the more qualified driver for a smoother ride and the well-being of the car.

Journey of Nafs to Perfection

STATIONS

Kamila (The Perfect Self)
Traits: Freedom from duality, acceptance of god's will, joy of union, freedom from expectation, contentment.
Habits: No remaining

Mardhiya (The Pleasing Self)
Traits: Knowledge of God, boundless faith and hope in existential communion.
Habits: Mystical intoxication, lack of sobriety

Radhiya (The Content Self)
Traits: Endurance, Resignation, constancy.
Habits: Personal identification with affliction

Mutmainna (The Tranquil Self)
Traits: Dignity, sincerity, courage, compassion, complete loyalty.
Habits: Attachment to spiritual ambition

Mulhimah (The Inspired Self)
Traits: Generosity, gratitude, modesty, empathy, zeal.
Habits: Liberality lacking, discrimination, mystical inflation, spiritual greed

Lawwama (The Reproachful Self)
Traits: Conscience, capacity for self-observation.
Habits: Backbiting, conceit, hypocrisy, self-consciousness guilt, fearfulness, wishful thinking, desire to please others

Ammara (The Animal Self)
Traits: Narcissistic, mechanical, conditioned, non-reflective, impulsive.
Habits: Pride, enmity, cruelty, lust, stinginess

Sufis believe that no man is absolutely bad or absolutely good. We are always inhabiting in some shades of grey; sometimes, it is closer to black and sometimes, it is closer to white. However, they do believe that man follows some sort of path in his journey to perfection after leaving his animalistic nature behind. This journey to perfection is characterised by certain behaviours and traits that can be roughly divided into seven stages that include the lowest stage being *Nafs-e-ammara* (the animal self) and the highest being *Nafs-e-kamila* (the perfect self), where the seeker can be declared a 'complete man'.

God Is an Experience

On the Sufi path, knowledge, reason, ritual, and everything else has its due place in the scheme of things, but the overall objective remains to bring you to the experience of God. If this objective is not met, the practitioner has the right to challenge and question any and all of these as they are no more than means to reach the destination. For a Sufi, rituals play an instrumental role and hence, should be need based and in accordance with the context.

Here's a hypothetical situation to substantiate this argument. Suppose a fire breaks out in your house and starts spreading across the house. As the owner of the house, what will be the most appropriate thing for you to do? Would you run away to a safer place immediately or sit and read a manual on 'How to put off fire' or go and shout for help or dial the fire helpline and until the fire brigade arrives, try to keep the fire under control by using the fire extinguisher available in the house? While all of these solutions have some merit, the utility of each is contextual. It can only be determined by visiting the real situation.

The first thing a seeker has to understand is that God or supreme consciousness is an experience. And thus, he has to see that where he stands vis-à-vis that experience, what resources he has at his disposal, and only after completely assessing the situation, take action (ritual) befitting his situation. We are all unique and therefore, what worked for somebody may not work for you the same way.

Certainty (*Yaqeen*)

According to most Sufi schools, a seeker's certainty in the existence of God passes through three stages:

a) *Ilm-ul-yaqeen*
b) *Ayn-ul-yaqeen*
c) *Haqq-ul-yaqeen*

These three stages can be roughly compared with reading about swimming, watching somebody swim, and the personal experience of being in water and swimming.

Knowledge of Certainty (*Ilm-ul-yaqeen*)

At this stage, the object of certainty is knowledge just as the aim of knowledge is certainty. This certainty is the first degree of spiritual life and the last of speculative experience.

Vision of Certainty (*Ayn-ul-yaqeen*)

The second degree of *yaqeen* is a consequence of contemplation and vision. At this level, the object of certainty is present before the gnostic and is not just a speculative concept. This kind of knowledge distinguishes the man of the 'way' from philosophers and learned men.

Certainty Gained through Experience (*Haqq-ul-yaqeen*)

Finally, the last degree of *yaqeen* is called *haqq-ul-yaqeen*, that is, certainty as supreme truth. It is the fruit of an all-embracing experience because the object of certainty is identical to the one who is experiencing it. In such an experience, knowledge transforms into an actual experience and vice versa. At this stage, knowledge is not limited to the intellect or the vision of the person who is contemplating it; it becomes one with the person.

Truth (*Haqq*)

There is a Sufi proverb, "It's not about what you call

it. It's about what it is." Caught in our belief systems and conditioning, what we manage to see is not the actual reality but rather a psychological reality or our image of reality. In such a state, we behave like a blind person who imagines the complete picture (the actual reality or truth) to be the limited portion of it he can sense through touch and sound. And in order to see the complete picture, we need to have the light which becomes available to us only when we learn to challenge our beliefs and imaginations (images about things from past memories) and break free from the shackles of conditioning. As the Bible says ". . . and the Truth will set you free."

This conditioning and limited impression of truth are beautifully illustrated in the well-known story of six blind men and an elephant.

Here, all the blind men are right in their claims but due to their limited capacity to perceive, they will never be able to see the complete elephant. Such is the difference between belief and truth.

Love (*Ishq*)

> *"It's easy to love a perfect God, who is unblemished and infallible that He is. What is far more difficult is to love fellow human beings with all their imperfections and defects. Remember, one can only know what one is capable of loving. There is no wisdom without love. Unless we learn to love God's creations, we can neither truly love nor truly know God."*
>
> — Shams Tabrīzī

To start with, it is important to understand that the love saints talk about is not the love we are familiar with. It resembles that love just a little and that too, just on the surface. The love we know is a good act, beneficial to the beloved, and creates a bond and attachment with the beloved's form. This love causes pain if the beloved is lost. On the other hand, the love Sufis are concerned with is not an act but a feeling or state which we may call a 'love state'. Here, the beloved is not a physical object (*ishq-e-majazi*) and hence, is beyond the scope of attachment. But here too, the lover faces pain, not of losing the beloved but of losing the connection with this state. According to Sufis, this state is achieved by decimating the *nafs* or weakening the ego and allowing our real self to be revealed. But it is easier said than done. It's considered such a difficult thing to do for a seeker that it's often compared to killing the self, or 'I'. As the following couplet by Kabir shows:

"Prem na kheto neepje prem na haat bikai.
Raja praja jehu ruche, sees dei lai jae."
(Lovc is neither cultivated in fields nor sold
in the marketplace.
Whether you are king or subject, give the
head and take it.)

Rumi puts love in the context of realising God in his following lines:

"Ishq asterlab-e-asrar-e-khuda ast."
(Love is the instrument which can gauge the
characteristics of God.)

The Hindu concept of *dwij* (born again) also comes from this idea of decimating the ego, which in other words, means returning to our essential nature of love, after dying to our conditioning. We are living in the twenty-first century and science has helped us understand a lot of phenomena that were undefined in earlier times. Some path-breaking research done by a few modern scientists may come handy in understanding the love the saints talked of.

700+	Enlightenment
600	Peace
540	Joy
500	Love
400	Reason
350	Acceptance
310	Willingness
250	Neutrality
200	Courage
175	Pride
150	Anger
125	Desire
100	Fear
75	Grief
50	Apathy
30	Guilt
20	Shame

David Hawkins explains that humans feel different states of being. Pride, shame, desire, courage . . . every feeling or emotion we experience makes our body vibrate at a specific frequency. The state of love is one of those frequencies at which we feel that we are in the flow and completely in sync with the rest of the universe.

Another scientist, Dr Leonard Horowitz, concludes: "A certain frequency resonates at the heart of everything that exists, and it connects our heart, our spiritual essence, to the spiralling reality of heaven and earth." Not only this, he further explains, "The DNA double helix vibrates at a specific resonant frequency which is 528 cycles per second," and this he terms as the 'love frequency'. He also observes that when our body vibrates at this frequency, it can remove impurities on its own, allowing itself to become healthy, balanced, and in the flow.

We have all felt that our body's vibration changes in accordance with our mental state and orientation. When we are happy and joyful, we feel lighter (higher frequency) and when we are sad, grieving, or ashamed, we experience a sinking feeling, a heaviness (lower frequency).

The saints agree that love is the best thing to dissolve the ego. Put in terms of David Hawkins's statechart: "Once you establish yourself in the state of 'Love', you are starting your journey to the higher frequencies of 'Joy', 'Peace' and 'Enlightenment'. In other words, weakening the 'Ego' and strengthening 'Love' is one and the same thing."

It is generally believed that to attain love, some hard work is required. This is far from the truth as work is required only to remove the blocks we have created against love . . . blocks of ego that don't allow us to live according to our true nature, as pointed out by Hazrat Waris Ali Shah, a late 19th-century saint from North India:

"Ishq wahi hai jo kasb se hasil nahin kiya ja sakta."

(Love is that which is not gained or acquired.)

This implies that the love state is our essential nature. It's our primordial state that we lose maybe right at the time of birth, as we become body conscious. After that, thanks to our further conditioning, indoctrinations, beliefs, and fears, we live our lives in 'I'-conscious state and seldom visit our primary nature which can be accessible to us only if we manage to get hold of pure consciousness.

To conclude, leaving our state and aligning with that of the better state of beloved, is the sole objective of the spiritual journey of the Sufis, as hinted very beautifully by Bulleh Shah:

"Ranjha ranjha kardi ve main aape ranjha hoyi. Ranjha ranjha saddo ni mainu Heer na aakho koyi . . ."

(Calling out for Ranjha for so long, I have myself become Ranjha. Call me Ranjha now, don't call me Heer anymore.)

Rumi professes something very similar about the divine love: "In this journey, the Lovers don't finally meet somewhere. They are in each other all along."

Duality Graph

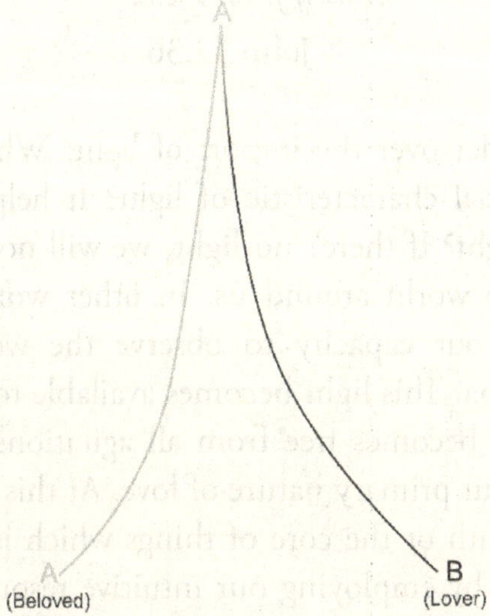

At the peak of this experience or realisation, the duality of the lover and beloved ends. Or in other words, both become perfectly aligned. In this state, the individual aligns himself in perfect harmony with the ultimate beloved supreme consciousness, and lives to his fullest potential, in peace and joy.

Observation (*Mushahida*)

God is called 'light' in many cultures and almost all the scriptures. The Bible, for example, says:

> *"'Believe in the light while you have the light, so that you may become children of light.' When he had finished speaking, Jesus left and hid himself from them."*
>
> — John 12:36

Let's ponder over the import of light. What is the most special characteristic of light? It helps us see things, right? If there's no light, we will not be able to see the world around us. In other words, light improves our capacity to observe the world and phenomena. This light becomes available to us once our mind becomes free from all agitations and we settle in our primary nature of love. At this level, we see the truth or the core of things which is beyond the form, by employing our intuitive resources and reflective capacity.

Here's an illustration to explain how our observation and perception improve as our consciousness grows. I leave it to the reader to reflect upon how this capacity to see beyond the obvious can improve your life and make you a better person.

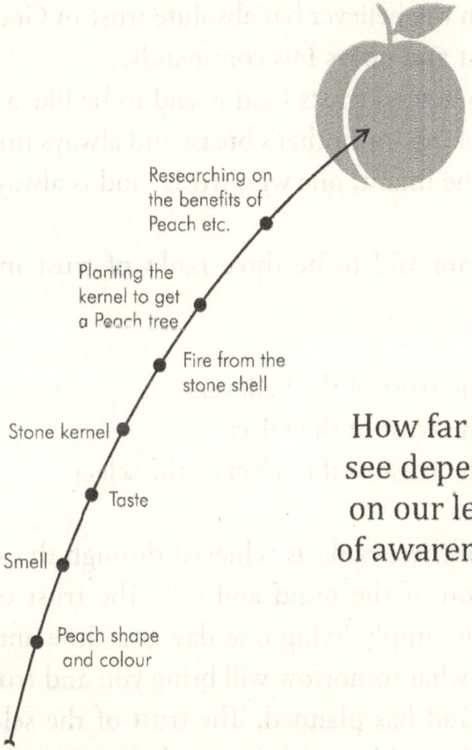

How far we see depends on our level of awareness.

Trust (*Tawakkul*)

Absolute trust in God and reliance on Him alone can be considered the most difficult attribute for the seeker to cultivate. Here, the seeker is expected to make the shift beyond the beneficiary–benefactor relationship with God to one where he believes that all that is coming from Him is for the seeker's greater good. In fact, the Quran teaches that success comes only when the believer has absolute trust in God and is steadfast and obeys His commands.

Someone who trusts God is said to be like a baby who is seeking its mother's breast and always finds it. Just like the infant, one who trusts God is always led to God.

There are said to be three ranks of trust in Sufi circles:

a) the trust of the believers
b) the trust of the select
c) the trust of the select of the select

Each of these ranks is achieved through the active reformation of the mind and self. The trust of the believers is simply living one day at a time and not worrying what tomorrow will bring you and trusting in what God has planned. The trust of the select is trusting God with no motives or desires. It is casting aside all wants. And finally, the trust of the select of the select is giving yourself over to God completely so that His desires become yours. In other words, trust in God is to be satisfied with God and by relying only on God, the highest. It is said that because God created everything and therefore, everything belongs to him, it is being selfish to want anything other than what God wishes or to not want something God provides you.

Balance (*Tawazun*)

By now we have understood that we don't have a fixed nature and our behaviour choices or actions are heavily dependent on our level of consciousness. Not only our choices but how much of the chosen thing is going to be good for us at that moment is also best decided by our awareness. This, of course, implies that a bad thing is bad for us, but even a good thing taken out of proportion can prove bad for us.

Let's take the example of your favourite dessert. A few scoops at the end of a meal is a healthy choice. On the other hand, if you greedily replace the rest of your meal with it, it can turn out to be an unhealthy decision. If you go further and start eating the dessert of your liking day in and day out, then that very source of pleasure can wreak havoc on your health.

Returning to our discussion, it's been proven that our ego is bad at striking this essential balance. More often than not, it overdoes what it likes. Sufis are of the opinion that man can't find this balance until his ego or lower self is weakened to the extent that it starts obeying the soul or higher self which is equipped with a better sense of balance. The Bhagavad Gita defines it as *stith pragya* which is the virtue of maintaining equilibrium in all situations.

Patience (*Sabr*)

Patience is a unique attribute of the Sufi way of life. It is not just acceptance of unavoidable and uncontrollable events with total trust and the belief that whatever is happening is happening for my good, but also an act as directed by God. As the Sufi surrenders everything to the divine, he not only accepts the divine will but also acts according to divine guidance. He acts only as much as is needed and beyond that he doesn't interfere with things, for often, no action is the best action.

At the core of Sufism, as has already been discussed, lies a relationship with the divine beyond the ordinary beneficiary–benefactor relationship. Thus, a seeker is ready to undergo experiences that outwardly may not seem beneficial in any sense. He treats them like a test by the divine, necessary to go through to be promoted to the next level. This is just like in academics where we are tested at the end of every grade for the level of our knowledge and understanding, before being promoted to a higher grade.

Let us take up an example to understand this. Suppose, a guru and disciple go on a very difficult journey to a far-off land. Here, the disciple can have patience with the guru only when he possesses full knowledge about the journey or wholeheartedly submits to the guru. If neither holds true, the disciple will remain impatient and hence be perpetually nagged by questions like how far have they reached, how many other possible routes are there to the destination, whether the path his guru has chosen is the most suitable one, etc. All these contribute to testing the patience of the disciple. By having patience with the guru, the disciple learns to have patience with the divine and hence exercises patience in every situation.

Once, Rabia Basri was in a discussion with another saintly figure of her time. Rabia asked him, "What is the sign of a true lover?" The saint replied, "He is someone who bears the trials of the beloved with a smile." Rabia corrected him, "No! A true lover is someone who doesn't even consider what the beloved apportions a trial." What Rabia is alluding to is the wonderful patience, *sabrun jamila*, that Sufis aspire to.

Intent (*Niyah*)

Intent, the Final Cause according to Aristotle's cause model, represents the 'why' of an action or behaviour. Sufis encourage their disciples to see things beyond the obvious (Formal cause) not only in the material world around them but even in their own actions and behaviour. They are prompted to probe the source, the intent behind their actions, and the actions of others, because one can easily be misled into believing a distorted reality at the outer level. For example, a mouse who can't see the intent behind the mouse trap sees the cheese, which is actually a bait, only as tempting food and nothing beyond it. So 'what' is being said or done matters less to a Sufi than 'why' it is being said or done. What you do is not as important to know, as to why you do it for a Sufi. Hence, it's the intent of the doer behind any action that is more important for the conscience and peace of the doer than the action itself. Ali-ibn-e-talib recommends:

"Never rely too much on your outer actions.
Focus on the intent behind those actions, for
you may show off in actions but not in intent."

Even when following socially approved rituals, which are commonly perceived to be pious and hence, beneficial, the Sufis advise caution before jumping on to the bandwagon. Their motto remains that if you don't know what you are doing and why you are doing, then please don't do it.

Again, it is the ego that is so obsessed with 'doing' that it more often than not undermines the 'being'. Interestingly, the intent lies in the being zone and therefore, the disciple is encouraged to observe actions (both his own and those of others) beyond what meets the eye and use his intuitive capacity to see the truth of the actions or intent behind these actions.

Integrity vs Etiquette (*Akhlaq-Tahzeeb*)

The world is full of traditions and customs, and though these socially accepted behaviours and etiquettes help the individual win the social approval, they are not very helpful in the spiritual domain which demands much deeper involvement from the seeker. When a seeker is seeking spiritual growth, he can't get away with actions or words that he doesn't own at the core. Spirituality is game of intent consciousness and if the individual doesn't mean what he is saying or doing, the action is deemed null and void or may even be counted as a foul that may, in the end, attract penalty and not reward. That is the reason why Sufis lay a lot of value on integrity which means to be being whole and complete. There is a popular saying that Sufi is a person whose intent, speech, and actions are perfectly aligned. This alignment facilitates the spiritual growth of the seeker to higher states.

The priority of integrity over etiquette is very beautifully captured in the following story of Mulla Nasruddin:

"Once, Mulla Nasruddin had been working in the fields all day long. He was hungry and tired, and his clothes were full of sweat from the day's hard work. On his way back home, he realised that he was invited to a feast that evening, and if he goes home to change then it may be too late to catch up the function. Hungry as he was, he decided to join the feast before going home.

When Nasruddin arrived, the wealthy host opened the door and looked at Nasruddin scornfully. Without a word of welcome, he gestured for Nasruddin to come in, and Mulla quietly settled in a corner, watching the throng of people, all dressed in their finest clothing, relishing all types of delicacies. Despite all his efforts, nobody tried to move over or make a space for Nasruddin. In fact, nobody offered him food. He had to make way through people to get food on his plate. Nobody spoke to him. Soon, Mulla felt so out of place and humiliated that after only a few bites, he decided to leave. He hurried home to change his clothing.

Dressed in finest of the clothes, Nasruddin returned to the feast, and this time, the host welcomed him with a huge smile, 'Welcome, welcome! Please come in.' As Nasruddin entered, people greeted and waved at him from all corners of the room as they invited him to sit near them. Everyone also offered him food. Nasruddin sat down quietly and while picking up different food items, he murmured, 'Eat, gown, eat.' He fed the gown bread, hummus, falafel, chicken and the various desserts that included halvah, date rolls, figs, and baklava!

Soon, everyone in the room was staring at Nasruddin. The host rushed to the spot where everybody was huddled to watch his strange behaviour. The host exclaimed, 'Nasruddin, what are you doing? Why are you behaving in this manner?'

'Well,' replied Nasruddin, 'when I first came to this feast in my old farming clothes, nobody welcomed me. No one would speak with me. But when I changed into this gown, suddenly I was greeted warmly. So, I realised that it was not me that was welcome at the feast, but my attire. And so, I am feeding my gown.'"

Transient vs Constant (*Fana–Baqa*)

It is important to recognise—as thinkers have advised over the ages—that 'the world is transient' and 'change is the only constant'. The Sufis profess that most of the trouble we face as humans is because we tend to treat the transient as a constant. We are not mentally prepared to accept change and hence, resist it, but ultimately fail and suffer heartache. So, the Sufis tell us not to attach ourselves to the fleeting (*fana*) which includes everything that exists and rather focus on the eternal (*baqa*) God. There's another way of looking at these two technical terms, *fana* and *baqa*, as transient and subsisting states respectively, to connote the annihilation of the human selfhood (the subjective self) in the sheer presence of God, which is *baqa*, where the human selfhood subsists as pure spirit (the objective self).

By discussing *fana* and *baqa* together, Sufis aim at putting across the point that the journey to God does not end in the annihilation of the self-awareness. Rather, the highest stage is where the human being is able to retain self-awareness while being fully aware of his true nature, the expansive state which they call love. This stage of subsistence after annihilation helps human beings live their earthly life in full harmony with God's will while retaining individual awareness that enables them to work, live with family, and guide others. Sufis regard this to be the state of prophet Muhammad (PBUH), a beautiful mix of worldly and divine.

A platform outside the house of a prophet in Madina used to be occupied with Sufi like figures hailing from all over the world, who would just be there to observe him coming and going. Such people were seldom seen openly mingling with him, unlike his other followers or recent converts, and were popularly known as *Ashab-e-suffa*.

Surrender (*Taslim*)

"Do what you want to do and you may never do what you can," warned a modern-day Sufi.

Man, when exercising his will, manages to make only limited use of his abilities and potential. But for a Sufi, being close to God means reaching a state of nothingness, whereby one becomes a fitting vehicle through which God may act as He wills. The point of Sufi training is not to gain in spirituality terms but to realise one's non-existence and thus, to better know and serve the One who exists.

In surrender, nothing needs to be proven and all things flow easily and naturally. The taste of surrender to the *murshid* is similar to the taste of surrender to God. In a fundamental sense, spiritual surrender does not have to be taken as something resulting in inaction or being in conflict with the effort to better ourselves and our surroundings. Acceptance does not mean that we should not or cannot contribute to the harmony and beauty of this world. On the contrary, one of the hallmarks of those who have surrendered to God is that such people are no longer motivated and driven by self-interest as it is this quality that not only brings them into conflict with others but also blocks the path of their surrender to the infinite. It goes without saying that it is only when we are not at war with ourselves and others that we become creative and sympathetic to others.

Sufis teach that as the individual surrenders his will to the will of God, his 'I'-centric or conditioned behaviour automatically gets replaced by his essential nature: love. Once this happens, his observation capacity improves like never before and a wide variety of choices of action open up which were earlier obscured and veiled from his sight. He not only has more choices to pick from but also has the ability to choose the most appropriate option. Hence, the strike rate of his actions improves tremendously. At his surrendered best, he becomes free of petty beliefs and conditioning and perfectly aligned with the truth.

Gratitude (*Shukr*)

Greed, the desire for ever more, is another hallmark of ego- or 'I'-centric life. It craves more and more sensual experiences that include exotic food, luxury, sensuality, social approval, longevity, money, children, etc. And the more it gets, the more it desires. It is never satiated or fulfilled as it is caught in this vicious cycle of chasing more, getting it, and then chasing for even more. As a pearl of popular wisdom puts it, "The cup of greed is never full."

Now, as the ego always feels that it has less than it should have by its own yardstick, it never thinks of being thankful for all that it has received. On the contrary, the soul is always content with whatever it gets and hence, it is more prone to expressing gratitude. To push the seeker from an egocentric life to a soul-centric one, Sufis recommend an attitude of gratitude as a transformative tool. Sufi poetry and instructive tales often recommend inculcating the attitude of gratitude to bring about a positive change in disciples. The following story illustrates this.

"One night, the angel of riches pays a visit to Mulla Nasruddin, the beggar, in a dream and ordered him to spread his cloak to collect the golden coins it had brought him to end his misery. The angel also warned that if the coins fell on the ground, they would turn into sand. Surprised and elated at the offer, Mulla spread his tattered cloak to receive the coins. The angel counted, 1, 2, 3 . . . and so on. At 25, the angel stopped and warned Mulla, 'If you take any more coins, your cloak may not be able to hold them.'

Instead of heeding this advice, Mulla countered the angel saying, 'Don't you worry! The cloak is really strong and can easily take more coins.' The angel started dropping the coins again: 26, 27 . . . and then whoosh! The cloak burst and the coins started turning to sand as they touched the ground. Mulla desperately tried to save the coins from falling but failed, and all the coins turned to sand right in front of his eyes. Mulla implored the angel to give him another chance, but the angel disappeared without saying a word, never to return."

Transformation, the Sufi way

"Rah e-suluk-e-ishq mein riyazat nahin zaroor;
sau- sau muqam hote hain tai, ek nigah mein."

(In the path of love, exercise is no compulsion; you may get elevated by 100 places in a single glance.)

The allopaths give tablets and perform surgery, the homoeopaths give sweet pills soaked in chemicals, and the Ayurveda doctors balance the *doshas* by administering herbs and juices. They all look very different in their techniques on the surface, but at the heart of their apparently widely divergent systems, they all are trying to achieve the same goal, i.e., to restore the health and balance of the patient and help him come out of the state of 'dis-ease'. Sufis, who are oriented to see the 'why' of actions, deem every ritual acceptable, provided it helps restore the primordial love state in the seeker. That's the reason why we find such a variety of rituals in the Sufi world and almost anything that a Sufi does qualifies as a ritual or transformative technique.

Respect of Soul for the Supreme (*Adab*)

At the outer level, *adab* is defined as respect. At a deeper level, it is an acknowledgement of the presence of God in one's thoughts, actions, and behaviour. When the soul is conscious of God, it behaves the way a child behaves in the presence of an elder: conscious out of humility, not fear. This is an essential attribute of Sufism which opens up the doors of grace for the seeker like no rituals or meditative practices can do. For if the seeker gets access to energies and higher spiritual capacities, as promised by most of the spiritual cults all over the world, without having the right attitude (*adab* or humility), then he may lose balance in the long run and get diverted from the path of spiritual grace.

In the present age, when our societies or economies are all about encouraging *nafs* (ego) by stoking desires, ambition, and selfish behaviour in the name of competition, a seeker may find it difficult to relate to this ego-negating attitude that helps the soul to flourish. When the seeker lives with this respect for the divine, he finds a natural way of being that nourishes his own soul and the souls of those in his environment. In a nutshell, *adab* helps us guard our being wherever we go. This way we learn to keep our ego on its toes all the time, not allowing it to drag us into *ghaflat* (negligence). Remember, that before we get negative, we go negligent.

The Master (*Murshid, sheikh, or peer*)

"Guru gobind dou khade, kake lagoon pae.
Balihari guru aapne, Gobind diyo batae."

(Guru and lord both are standing together.
Who should I adore first?
O' Guru, you are greater who told me that
God is the greatest.)

The above quote by Kabir, a 15th-century Indian mystic, captures the transformation formula of the Sufis . . . if at all there is any. The Sufis believe that man is an amalgam of knowledge, state, and action. The *sheikh* (teacher), who is stationed at a higher plane in terms of all these three elements, poses as a role model for the disciple, as far as his spiritual quest is concerned. Partly through the induced stimulation by the *sheikh* and partly through inspiration, reflection, and emulation of the *sheikh*, the disciple improves and develops his finer faculties in due course of time, depending upon his capacity and the competence of the *sheikh*. The relationship between disciple and *sheikh* is a very unusual and indefinable one. It is very difficult to find a parallel of this relationship among other similar associations that exist in society.

There is no fixed formula that can be prescribed to the disciple to ensure his spiritual growth. Sometimes, the *sheikh* might give him deep philosophical lessons, sometimes he may share inspirational stories, and at other times, he might teach him through breath meditation, chants, dance, music, demonstrations . . . just about anything you can imagine. But on close observation, you will find an underlying method to all that the *sheikh* does as in the case of doctors. The *sheikh* treats the interventions and activities like instruments or tools and uses them selectively, keeping the objective of transformation and growth of the disciple in mind. He uses these techniques like medication and controls their dose and duration solely depending upon the sickness of the patient.

In fact, a *sheikh* performs three roles we are familiar with in the world of medicine: diagnosis (pathology lab), prescription (physician), and supplying medicine (pharmacist). And if the patient cannot be cured at that moment, even after all the three have been applied, the *sheikh* waits for the right moment to intervene.

In the presence of the *sheikh* or *sohbet*, the student gets a chance to learn not only from his spoken word (*qaul*) but also from his actions (*amal*), like an apprentice cook learns from his senior chef by watching him chop vegetables, fry onion, pick spices, and serve the dish. Rumi expresses this beautifully in the following couplet:

"Yaq zamana sohbat-e-ba Auliya
Behtar az sad saala Ta'at-e-be riya."
(A moment spent in the company of a true saint is better than a hundred years of worship with a pure heart.)

What he is saying is that it's better to spend a moment with a master chef (*sheikh*) than to struggle alone in the kitchen for years to learn a thing or two about cooking.

Ego (*Nafs*)

At the heart of the essentials of transformation in the Sufi path is *nafs*, which can be loosely translated in English as the ego, the 'I'-consciousness, or the conditioned self.

Some Sufi schools treat *nafs* as one of the two centres of orientation in humans and term it as the ego-centre or the lower self, which is different from the soul-centre or the higher self. The lower self operates from fear; fear of losing the comfort of the body, fear of losing the image of the 'I' it mistakes for the real self, and fear of loss of everything it has accumulated and attached itself to. On the contrary, the higher self is more expansive and operates from love.

Other schools liken *nafs* to dirt and sticky dust covering the clear mirror of the soul (*ruh*). It, therefore, obscures its reflective capacity and renders it ineffective for showing the truth which, in turn, blocks humans from operating from their true nature of love. The dust and stains that gather on the surface of the soul (the soul being the only centre according to this school) are nothing but stain-like impressions we keep leaving on the clear mirror of the soul from the moment of our birth and which cumulatively adds up as we grow. These stains are our identity, sense organ memories, concepts, prejudices, beliefs, conditioning, experiences, feelings, attachments, desires, cravings, and habits. The stronger our attachment to these stains, the greater their stubbornness.

Whether *nafs* is viewed as a separate centre of orientation or as dirt obscuring the mirror of the soul, cleansing of these undesirable attributes of *nafs* (*tazkiya-an-nafs*) is considered the primary task for a Sufi seeker. As he succeeds in incapacitating his lower self, his higher self is revealed to him in the same proportion.

Sufis give the analogy of horse training to explain *tazkiya-an-nafs*. If a horse is not trained, it will be impossible for a rider (soul) to ride it smoothly. Erratically driven by the *nafs* our body, senses, mind, and other faculties, we behave like a wild horse which would go wherever it wants to. Once *nafs* is systematically tamed, our intuitive capacity (heart) and finer extrasensory perceptions take control of our body and senses. This can be compared to a trained horse which moves in accordance with the commands of the rider (soul/heart), allowing the animal's potential to be put for a more productive use.

To conclude, let me list some attributes of *nafs* put together by Sufi thinkers over the ages. By working against these undesirable tendencies, we can purify ourselves and progress along the spiritual path. I recommend starting by working on the one that you most strongly relate to and, in due course of time, you will notice many other minor negative attributes in the list will gradually start losing their grip on you.

Common Blemishes of the *Nafs* (Ego)*

We must come out of the darkness of heedlessness to see if we have the traces of these maleficent traits. These are the veils of heedlessness that we must identify and lift.

* Credit: www.jerrahi.org

- Arrogance of one's false spiritual state.
- Hypocrisy of appearing as one is not.
- Pride of one's false evaluation of oneself.
- Envy of that which is not one's due.
- Stinginess in wishing to keep all that has been given by God.
- Vengeance by assuming oneself as the judge and executioner.
- Infidelity and betrayal of trust.
- Heresy—exchanging truth for falsehood.
- Thanklessness—the inability to value things.
- Being a complainer and dissatisfied with one's lot.
- Hopelessness—a refusal to believe in God's mercy.
- Cynicism—being certain only of God's punishment.
- Tyranny or being a sympathiser with tyrants.
- Destructive criticism, especially of the faithful and those on the straight path.
- Attachment to the world and detaching oneself from the truth.
- The desire to be a leader.
- The desire to be praised.
- The fear of being abased.
- The need for amusement.
- Insincere imitation.
- Abasing oneself to obtain worldly benefits.

- Enjoying the suffering of one whom one takes as an enemy.
- Being a coward.
- Being negative.
- Obtaining what one desires through injustice.
- Being untrustworthy and not keeping one's word.
- Being superstitious.
- Thinking ill of other people.
- Love of and attachment to one's property.
- Spending all of one's efforts for the worldly pleasures.
- Being over-ambitious.
- Being irresponsible.
- Being a workaholic.
- Delaying what must be done.
- Being shameless and without conscience.
- Not knowing the value of time.
- Despairing in worldly failures and in loss of position or property.
- Backbiting.
- Stubbornness.
- Egoism.
- Being boastful.
- Cheating.
- Rudeness.
- Lustfulness.
- Lack of respect for others.

- Refusal to accept any fault.
- Fear of poverty.
- Disbelief in faith.
- Being a defeatist.
- Taking pleasure in belittling others.
- Refusal to take anything seriously.
- Being a flatterer of the rich and powerful.
- Disdain for the meek.
- Pride in one's history.
- Bravado.
- Being nonsensical.
- Talking too much and never listening.
- Ignoring one's faults and being preoccupied with the faults of others.
- The absence of the fear of God in one's heart.
- Curing one's dissatisfaction by feeding one's ego.
- Not assisting in the protection of what is due to God and to His creation.
- Being two-faced and dishonest.
- Taking pleasure in other people's misfortune.
- Not accepting the punishment for one's wrongdoings.

You may be outwardly pious or saintly but be sure that you are operating from your *Nafs* (ego)/lower self, if you are:

- Not able to save your worship from the distortion of your imaginations.
- Gathering in congregations not to listen to the truth, but to listen to the noise or get entertained.
- Spending your energy to impress others while ignoring your own spiritual needs.
- Interested in the company of women, youth, and pleasant friends and love to listen to others talk about you.
- Taking social traditions as the principles of the religion because you are lax or impressed by anything you hear.
- Liking the noise of jokes and laughter to the truth because you follow what pleases you.
- Pleasing others instead of your soul, for you have turned your back to the truth.
- Keen on pushing your own idea of truth (belief) to be accepted as the truth.
- Making a show of your deeds and demanding recognition, while not doing a single thing.
- Always in a hurry to achieve goals which you have set for yourself without setting yourself conditions or abiding by any rules.
- Thinking that you can fool everyone, often including yourself.
- Fond of lauding your spiritual practices.

- Devoid of compassion and the ability to forgive.
- Unable to respect or have consideration for fellow humans.

Demonstration (*Daleel*)

What can't be written in books or explained in words can best be taught by demonstration. Truth is like the sun, best experienced and not read or talked about. The following story about Bahlol Dana is a good example of teaching by demonstration.

"One night, a reputed scholar of Baghdad was discussing some deep philosophical topics with his students. The students surrounded the teacher as the teacher went about boasting, 'Today, I would like to discuss three things that I disagree with my teacher about:

a) My teacher says that Satan will be punished in the fires of hell. However, since Satan is made of fire, how can fire hurt fire?
b) He says God exists, but we can't see Him. How is that possible; if something exists, it must also be seen.
c) He says we are responsible for our actions, but if God controls everything in the universe then why should man be punished for his actions?

Is there anyone who can answer these questions?'

Standing next to the window was Bahlol Dana, the wise fool. He was listening to each and every word of this arrogant teacher. The teacher had barely completed his statement when a stone whirling through the darkness hit him on the forehead and he cried out in pain, 'Seize him!'

The students ran out of the room towards the window. They ran a distance and chased Bahlol who was running away from the scene. 'Okay! Okay! I give up. What do you want?' enquired Bahlol. The scholar ordered his students to take him to the caliph so that he could seek justice.

The caliph knew Bahlol and his ways. The moment he saw him in court, he exclaimed, 'Bahlol, what have you done now?'

The scholar pleaded, 'Your highness, I have been wronged. This man hurt me with a stone for no fault of mine, while I was having a discussion with my students. I couldn't sleep the whole night due to pain.'

The caliph asked, 'Did you hurt this man Bahlol?'

'Yes, but I was only answering his questions!' replied Bahlol instantly.

'Answering someone's questions by hitting them with stones?' screamed the caliph, annoyed by this strange logic.

Bahlol thought a while and then spoke, looking at the scholar, 'Hurt? Pain? I don't see any hurt or pain. Can you please show me your pain, dear sir? I did not know pain could be seen.'

The scholar felt insulted at this remark and he thundered, 'Are you insane? You fool, don't you know that pain can only be felt and not seen.'

'Exactly, just as God exists even though He can't be seen by the naked eye,' reasoned Bahlol.

'Also sir, just as the stone made of earth can cause pain to you, a being also made of earth, the fire of hell can punish Satan who's created from fire. And lastly, why have you brought me into the presence of his highness? You should have brought in God, after all. He's responsible for all that happens in the universe, isn't it, sir?' The scholar realised his mistake and thanked Bahlol for teaching him this lesson.

Service (*Khidmat*)

'If you wish to serve the beloved, you should serve others' is the main motto of the Sufis. Only in selfless service, we begin to see ourselves clearly. Through the acts of service, the rough ego starts to be smoothened and we learn to be humble, tender, and loving. Harsh judgements, arrogance, and divisive qualities get diluted in the rivulet of our intentions to help others. The two legs of Sufism are selfless service and love as only one who loves can truly serve. The Sufi is a lover of God, and like any other lover, he proves his love by constant remembrance and service of His beloved's creation. Sufis are known for their contribution to the general good of society by running hermitages, schools, *langars* (feeding the masses), playing advisors to kings, and speaking up for the rights of the poor and needy. Many Sufis have also penned poems and composed music, while some have given lectures and taught meditation and folklores which are full of stories of miracles performed by the Sufis in their local communities. Not only that, but some Sufis have also contributed to the making of social laws and have also played *qazi* (judge) apart from teaching spirituality to the seekers. They have always contributed to society in more ways than actually acknowledged by their societies. For Sufis, the true practice of devotion is service, and what better can someone give to the world than giving the best version of himself?

Dream (*Khwab*)

The dream world is an important part when it comes to higher guidance. When we sleep, we return to our primordial nature and it is an effective time for spiritual growth, healing, and restoration. We become innocent when we sleep and when we awaken, we may have clear answers to many of life's challenges. The ancient Sufis are said to have turned to their dreams for guidance, clarity, and wisdom. Dream is deemed to be an important tool to help us in our spiritual journey. The Sufi approach to dream science is to share the dreams with the *sheikh* who can provide a divine interpretation of your dreams, rather than relying on third party interpretations with whom the disciple doesn't cherish any spiritual connection. Here's a story to illustrate the significance that Sufis place on dreams in their paths of spiritual progress. This story consists of a dream reported from the life of great 11th-century Sufi, Imam Abu Hamid al-Ghazali. It is said that Al-Ghazali was beset by many personal struggles of spiritual nature during certain phases of his religious studies. Though he was doing very well as a scholar, he was not very content with what he learnt from philosophy and books.

One day he, had a dream in which he had a conversation with God, wherein he was told to 'abandon his formal rules' and to join the company of the Sufis whom he had been questioning for their informal attitude. He requested God to help him change his feelings toward them. In response, he was assured that the change will be made and that he will receive new 'lights' for his protection. When he awoke from the dream in great joy, Imam Ghazali reported it to his *sheikh*, who gave further explanation of the dream. This dream is said to be a turning point in Al-Ghazali's life and career and one of the factors that led to his turn toward Sufism from orthodox Islam.

Take some time to remember your dreams and how they make you feel when you awaken and deepen your understanding of the wisdom that is coming through in your dream state. There is saying among Indian Sufis, "Until you find a *guru*, watch your dreams, for the dreams are half *guru*."

Observation of the State (*Muraqaba*)

Muraqaba is a unique Sufi expression of meditation. It is a visualisation technique where the student tries to emulate the state of his *sheikh* by merging his own inferior state (*hal*) with the persona of the *sheikh*. The chief purpose of *muraqaba* is to comprehend the spiritual mysteries of self and the universe and to experience an eternal life in union with God. Every human being experiences two states when they are alive. One of these conditions or state is waking and the other is sleeping or dreaming. In the waking state, they are bound by time and space, while during dreaming, they are free from the confines of spatiotemporal limitations. This freedom from time and space is consciously sought through *muraqaba* by converting the state of sleeping or dreaming into an awakened state. As during *muraqaba*, a person goes through the same conditions that he or she goes through while sleeping or dreaming. Here the pupil sits in the position for *namaz* and imagines the *sheikh* sitting opposite to him and visualises himself merging into the *sheikh*. It is a popular meditation technique prescribed in many Sufi orders all across the world.

Muraqaba improves memory, mental concentration, and boost the spiritual energy of the individual. You feel good and appear glowing by the mystic enlightenment of *muraqaba*. It can help you to advance special abilities like extrasensory perception and clairvoyance as well. But this practice may also temporarily cause uncertainty, perplexity, depression, anxiety, and other psychological disorders in the individual.

Seclusion vs Company (*Khalwat–Sohbet*)

Sitting in seclusion for certain prescribed periods to observe the breath, thoughts, desires, intent, assumptions, beliefs, and everything that limits the seeker from realising the truth is encouraged among the disciples in varying degrees, depending on their stations. Dervishes often retire to the mountains, jungles and caves for the purpose of contemplation and introspection.

Broadly, seclusions are of two types. One is the outward kind in which the seeker, far from people, sits alone at a secluded place, shunning all contacts from the world. As a result, his external senses withdraw themselves and the inner senses (intuition) extend themselves to receive signals from the spiritual world. The second kind of retreat is the inward type, where the seeker inwardly witnesses the real or truth even while being outwardly surrounded by people. It's called *khalwat dar anjuman* (seclusion in the crowd) and means to be outwardly with people and inwardly to be with God. One of the saints has described this state as being so constantly and completely absorbed in divine remembrance that one could walk through the marketplace without hearing a word.

On the other hand, sticking to the Sufi formula of discontinuity, there may come a time when the seeker may be in a position to benefit from the *sohbet* (company) of like-minded people in order to learn, apply his learning, and share with them what he has learnt.

Travel (*Safar*)

The ego loves attachment, comfort, inertia, status quo, and habituation but hates the unknown. If the seeker encourages any of these qualities, he will invariably consolidate his *nafs.* His love for inertia acts like a roadblock when it comes to shifting to a soul-centric life. Popularly termed, 'The journey to home', these travels are in fact trips from a world of illusion to a world of reality. The wayfarer travels from the world of creation to the world of the Creator. In other words, travel from the human attributes toward the angelic qualities or moving from blameworthy qualities to laudable ones. There are records highlighting the fact that whenever the wayfarers became established in a place, got accustomed to it, and became familiar with its people, they took on travelling in order to break down habit and comfort and cut themselves off from fame. They would choose to travel in order to experience purging of 'I', by witnessing its limitations. There have been Sufis who were known for never living at a place for more than forty days throughout their active life.

Attention (*Tawwajjo*)

The latest research findings reveal that a powerful gaze has the capacity to change the heartbeat and hence, the state of the person being looked at. It has always been an effective transformative tool in the Sufi armoury. A *sheikh* can impart the state directly by his gaze or hug to a disciple who is in a state of readiness, without any exchange of words or a ritual. According to tradition, one day the Prophet (PBUH) was holding the hand of Umar, the second caliph of Islam. Umar said to him, "O' Allah's apostle! You are dearer to me than anyone except my own self."

The Prophet said, "No, by Him in whose hand my soul is, you will not have complete faith until I am dearer to you than your own self."

Then, only a moment later, Umar said to him, "However, now by Allah, you are dearer to me than my own self."

The Prophet said, "Now, O' Umar, now you are a believer." This was, without doubt, the result of direct transmission.

Fasting (*Roza*)

Sufism, in general, believes in the material to the spiritual journey. It is considered to be important for the basic groundwork that is needed before the initiate can be engaged in finer exercises to elevate his state to higher levels. What is the use of good knowledge if the body remains addicted to bad habits? Sooner or later, it will overpower the knowledge and make it do what it is habituated with doing, while the consciousness will only helplessly watch it happen, with no willpower to resist the unhealthy action. Fasting is prescribed to disciples, especially in the early stages, to gain command over their body and senses. This exercise helps the initiate fight his animalistic or carnal desires and be more focused and at ease when it comes to performing other exercises in the next stage. The following story illustrates the virtues of fasting.

"Once, in the pre-automobile era, a saintly figure came to pay a visit to a hermitage. From his attire, he looked like the native of some far-off land, but he was on foot and surprisingly fresh looking. A volunteer at the hermitage received him and enquired where he had come from. The visitor named a place which was hundreds of kilometres away. The answer shocked the volunteer. He thought, 'How can somebody travel such a distance in such a short time on foot. I will definitely ask for the secret behind this amazing capacity whenever next I get a chance to speak to this man.' A few days later, when the visitor decided to leave, the same volunteer tagged along to see him off. As they were coming out of the hermitage together, the volunteer found that he had to run to keep pace with the saintly figure strolling comfortably. While running, he asked: 'What is the secret behind this?'

Picking up further pace, the saint looked at the scrambling volunteer and smilingly murmured, 'As the body gets nourishment from food, the soul gets nourishment from not eating food.' After this, the volunteer could no longer keep pace with the visitor and fell back. In a few moments, he saw the visitor disappear from sight."

Chants/Remembrance (*Dhikr*)

Chanting in which the worshipper is absorbed in the rhythmic repetition of the names of God or his attributes, helps shift the vibration of the body, which facilitates a shift in the state of the engaged chanter. The chants are prescribed by the *sheikh* after assessing the need and readiness of the disciple. Every chant, name of God, and mantra has a specific effect on the state of the chanter and hence, should not be prescribed universally, barring a few generic exercises that may be considered beneficial for all.

Whirling (*Sema, Raqs*)

Sama is a means of meditating on God by focusing on melodies and dancing. Sufi whirling is a form of dynamic meditation which traces its origin to the Sufis of Persia and Turkey. It was popularised by the dervishes of the Mevlevi order (founded by the followers of Rumi in Turkey). The story of the creation of this unique form of *dhikr* is that once Rumi was walking through the town marketplace when he heard the rhythmic hammering of the goldbeaters. It is believed that Rumi heard the *dhikr, la ilaha ilallah* (there is no god but Allah), in the apprentices' beating of the gold and became so entranced in happiness that he stretched out both of his arms and started spinning in a circle (Sufi whirling). Through this ritual, which is seen as a symbolic imitation of planets in the solar system orbiting the sun, the *samazen* (performer) aims to reach the source of all perfection (*kamal*) by abandoning his *nafs* or personal desires, by listening to music, focusing on God, and spinning his body in repetitive circles. In Egypt, the Mevlevi form of *sama* is known as *tannoura* and it has been adopted (with some modifications) by other Sufi orders as well. It is also performed as a folk and concert dance.

Singing (*Sama, Qawl*)

Sama is a well-known form of Sufi music common in South Asia. It is also known as *qawwali* (root word *qawl*, which means to speak) which is a form of Sufi devotional music notably popular in the Punjab and Sindh, Hyderabad, and north India. Though *qawwali* is said to have been introduced by Khwaja Moinuddin Chishti, the famous saint of Ajmer (India), Delhi's Sufi saint Amir Khusrow is credited with fusing the Persian, Arabic, Turkish, and Indian musical traditions in the late 13th century in India to create *qawwali* as we know it today. The formal name used for a session of *qawwali* is *mehfil-e-sama*.

The central theme of this unique vocal and instrumental work is love, devotion, and longing of a seeker for the beloved or God. *Qawwali* is characterised by high-decibel singing coupled with subtle pointers to higher consciousness. *Sama* is the devotional music of the Sufis, inspired by the works of Sufi poets like Rumi, Hafiz, Bulleh Shah, Amir Khusrow, and Khwaja Ghulam Farid. The songs which constitute the qawwali repertoire are primarily in Persian, Urdu, Hindi, Bengali, and Punjabi and dialects of north India like Braj Bhasha and Awadhi. Actually, Sufis from Indonesia to Afghanistan and

Morocco to Azerbaijan have made music central to their devotional rituals in one form or the other.

Literature (*Tasnif/Taleef*)

Stories are a powerful tool to put people in a reflective mode and teach them values in a subtle manner by bypassing the reasoning mind. Stories of the Bible, Quran, Mahabharata, and Ramayana have been a source of inspiration and transformation for readers and believers since time immemorial. The Sufis have also written books, stories, couplets, and poems that carry profound wisdom and help the seekers learn, reflect, and move to the next level of consciousness. Following are some exemplar literary work of Sufis.

- ***The Masnavi* by Rumi***

The Masnavi, started by Rumi in the final years of his life, is a poetic collection of anecdotes and stories derived from the Quran, Hadith (prophet's sayings/traditions) sources, and everyday tales. Stories are told to illustrate a point and each moral is discussed in detail. It incorporates a variety of Islamic wisdom but primarily focuses on emphasising inward personal Sufi interpretation. In contrast to Rumi's Diwan, the six-volume Masnavi is a relatively 'sober' text. It explains the various dimensions and practices of spiritual life to Sufi disciples and anyone who wishes to ponder the meaning of life.

The six books of the Masnavi can be divided into three groups of two because each pair is linked by a common theme. Books 1 and 2 are principally concerned with the *nafs* (lower carnal self), and its self-deception and evil tendencies. Books 3 and 4 share the principal themes of reason and knowledge. The last two books (books 5 and 6) are joined by the universal ideal that man must deny his physical earthly existence to understand God's existence.

- ***The Revival of the Religious Sciences* by Al-Ghazali***

Ihyā' 'Ulūm al-Dīn is an 11th-century book written by Imam Ghazali. The book was composed in Arabic and was based on personal religious experience. Ghazali, at the peak of his fame and scholarship, went into a spiritual and intellectual crisis. He left his post at the institution to embark on a pilgrimage. His long journey consisted of travelling to Damascus, Jerusalem, and then finally, to Mecca. Throughout his journey, Ghazali was going through an inner spiritual struggle, and he became attracted towards the pathway of Sufis.

This work's great accomplishment was to bring orthodox Islamic theology and Sufi mysticism together in a useful and comprehensible manner. It's said that "Were the books of Islam all to be lost, excepting only the *Ihya*, it would suffice to replace them all."

- ***Kashf-ul-Mahjoob* by Ali Hujwiri***

Kashf-ul-Mahjoob, which translates to 'unveiling the veiled', is one of the most ancient and revered Persian treatises on Sufism and contains a complete system of Sufism with its doctrines and practices. The book also highlights many mystical controversies and clarifies a lot of floating contemporary opinions.

In this book, Ali Hujwiri, who was a renowned Sufi saint of his time, adopts an expository approach to define Sufism. He states that in this age, people are only obsessed with seeking pleasure and not interested to satisfy their need of higher consciousness. The following is an extract from his book:

"Theologians have made no distinction between *ilm* (knowledge) and *ma'arifat* (gnosis) . . . One, then, who knows the meaning and reality of a thing they call *arif* and one who knows merely the verbal expression and keeps it in his memory without keeping the spiritual reality, they call him *alim*. Sufis do not blame the man for having acquired knowledge, rather they blame him for neglecting the practice of religion because the *alim* depends on himself, but the *arif* depends on his Lord."

This work is treated as a textbook of Sufism. Even Khwaja Moinuddin Chishti, who was a chief saint of India, once stated that an aspiring *murid* (disciple) should read Ali Hujwiri's book, *Kashf-ul-Mahjoob*, until he finds a *murshid* (guru) as that would—temporarily—guide him spiritually. Originally written in Persian almost millennia ago, this book has been translated into various languages across the world.

- ***The Conference of the Birds* by Farid-ud-Din Attar***

Mantiq-ut-Tayr or *The Conference of the Birds* is a celebrated literary masterpiece of Persian literature by Sufi poet, Farid-ud-Din Attar. In the poem, the birds of the world gather to decide who is to be their sovereign as they have none. The hoopoe, the wisest of them all, suggests that they should find the legendary Simorgh and leads the birds, each of whom represents a human fault which prevents humankind from attaining enlightenment.

The hoopoe tells the birds that they have to cross seven valleys in order to reach the abode of Simorgh. These valleys are as follows:

1. Valley of the Quest, where the wayfarer begins by casting aside all dogma, belief, and unbelief.
2. Valley of Love, where reason is abandoned for the sake of love.
3. Valley of Knowledge, where worldly knowledge becomes utterly useless.
4. Valley of Detachment, where all desires and attachments of the world are given up. Here, what is assumed to be 'reality' vanishes.
5. Valley of Unity, where the wayfarer realises that everything is connected and that the beloved is beyond everything, including harmony, multiplicity, and eternity.
6. Valley of Wonderment, where, entranced by the beauty of the beloved, the wayfarer becomes perplexed and, steeped in awe, finds that he or she has never known or understood anything.
7. Valley of Poverty and Annihilation, where the self disappears into the universe and the wayfarer becomes timeless, existing in both the past and the future.

The following is an extract from his book:

"When the birds hear the description of these valleys, they bow their heads in distress; some even die of fright right then and there. But despite their trepidations, they begin the great journey. On the way, many perish of thirst, heat, or illness, while others fall prey to wild beasts, panic, and violence. Finally, only thirty birds make it to the abode of Simorgh. In the end, the birds learn that they themselves are the Simorgh; the name Simorgh in Persian means thirty-birds (*si-morgh*). They eventually come to understand that the majesty of that beloved is like the sun that can be seen reflected in a mirror. Yet, whoever looks into that mirror will also behold his or her own image."

The parables in this book trigger memories deep within us all. The stories inhabit the imagination, and slowly, over time, their wisdom trickles down into the heart. The process of absorption of these values is unique to every individual. We are the birds in the story. All of us have our own ideas and ideals, our own fears and anxieties, as we hold on to our own version of the truth. Like the birds of this story, we may take flight together, but the journey itself will be different for each of us.

Attar tells us that truth is not static, and that we each tread a path according to our own capacity. It evolves as we evolve. Those who are trapped within their own dogma, clinging to hardened beliefs or faith, are deprived of the journey toward the unfathomable Divine, which Attar calls the Great Ocean.

(*Source: Wikipedia)

Apart from the above-mentioned texts, 'Heer Ranjha', 'Laila Majnu', and stories of Mulla Nasruddin and Bahlol Dana (the wise fool of Baghdad) are other popular Sufi writings that are still considered timeless masterpieces and have been translated into different languages across the world.

Chapter 3

Roadblocks to Spiritual Growth

It goes without saying that spiritual progress demands self-discipline and a lot of courage. It is about challenging your fake self (ego) to access real self (soul), but this is a tough nut to crack, as many seekers would vouch for. Interestingly, we are living in societies that are obsessed with sensual gratification and hence, the spiritual practices which advise you otherwise are promptly repelled by the popular belief system. People have become so easy on themselves that they would rather go for a healing session than sit for meditation. We are so preoccupied with hedonism that we try to avoid anything that demands endurance or being a little tough with ourselves. Consequently, being sensual today is like swimming with the stream and being spiritual is like swimming against the flow.

In the absence of spiritual culture, the spiritual quest is more or less an individual venture. And many who fiddle with the spiritual tools hoping that they may fetch them quick-fix happiness and peace don't take their spiritual growth very seriously. The following verse by Kabir drops a few hints for such individuals and our society at large:

"Kami krodhi lalchi, inse bhakti na hoye.
Bhakti karai koi surma, jati varan kul khoye."

(The lustful, angry, or greedy cannot have devotion.
Only a valiant who has sacrificed caste, creed, and race can have devotion.)

If spirituality is the journey to our core, then the roadblocks on this journey also lie deep within us—in our attitudes, concepts, beliefs, and conditioning. Though this topic deserves a separate book, I would like to, at least, touch upon this important aspect as I don't find many spiritual modalities addressing this in very clear terms. Here, are a few common roadblocks I have come across in my journey as a seeker and observed in people as a coach.

Intellectualism

Most of us start our spiritual quest with books. These days, books have been partly replaced by search engines, videos, and online spiritual lectures. Knowledge is a good start, but it's a means to reach something real and is not an end in itself. For example, a travel brochure may trigger a journey, but it can't take you anywhere on its own. If you reflect upon this approach, you will realise that when we cannot experience something we are deeply interested in, we start by googling, reading about it, watching videos, listening to talks on it, and so on. But all this is of no use if we don't move to the next level—experiencing it first-hand. Higher consciousness is not knowledge or an intellectual quest; it's an experience, a feeling, a state. Here's a small incident to highlight this.

"Sometime during the British rule in India, a learned man came from Kabul to Dewa (a town in Barabanki district near Lucknow) to meet Haji Waris Ali Shah, a famous saint of the subcontinent in those days. When he met the saint, he asked a few typical questions which the great saint offered to answer the next day. When everybody went to sleep in the night, the visitor, instead of sleeping, chose to read Rumi's Masnavi and recite it aloud. The next day, before he was ready to meet the saint, he heard the saint asking, 'Who was reading Rumi's Masnavi in the night?'

Somebody replied, 'It was the same learned guest who was there asking questions yesterday.'

The saint remarked, 'Tell him to reflect upon what he reads.'"

In today's time and age, when we are flooded with content. Intellectualism can be a deadly trap which can block the real experience. One should be very watchful of it.

Emotionalism

Emotions can be employed to help the seeker ascend to the spiritual zone and shift state. But regulating emotions is a fine art that only the masters know. On the other hand, ritualists, who just have the tools and no craftsmanship, may end up doing more damage than good. If overdone or not properly administered, emotional charge—be it from chants, music, or dance—will make the seeker addicted to the ritual, forcing him to crave more and more of emotional kicks while remaining stuck at the same state or sliding to a lower spiritual level. Seekers may spend their lives enjoying overexposure to these entertaining rituals that may bring about positive transformation only if used effectively as an instrument.

Social Approval

I come across many people who are so obsessed with the exotic that they would rather attend a spiritual retreat on a private island and spend a huge amount on what they could have easily found for one-tenth the price at an island in Lakshadweep or a quiet Himalayan spot. There are a lot of seekers who join prestigious cults, ashrams, and exotic enlightenment clubs. But the primary question is: what are they seeking and why are they seeking it? If they stop to think about it, they may be able to confess to themselves that their aims consist of just doing something that is socially aspirational rather than for seeking anything spiritual. In fact, they are actually trying to satisfy the social approval need of their ego by giving it an acceptable name. As the Sufi saying goes, "It's not what you call it . . . it's what it is."

Ritualism

Rituals can be defined as a series of actions done regularly. I was talking to a saint sometime back, and he shared a beautiful story about how rituals are born and why they are not always reliable.

"Once there was a guru who would perform pooja every evening, where he would offer *kheer* (rice pudding) to the deity and sing hymns along with his disciples. There was a young kitten in the ashram who loved *kheer*, as most cats do. Finding everybody busy singing with eyes closed, the kitten would often sneak through the gathering and lap up the *kheer* offered to the god. This would force the guru to repeat the pooja. After this happened a few times, the guru devised a solution. He would order the cat to be chased and tied to a tree next to them before starting the pooja and then everything would go smoothly.

A few years later, the cat grew old and died. Coincidently, the day the cat died, the guru was not in the ashram. That day, no pooja happened in the ashram. The next day, when the guru came back and came to know that no pooja had taken place in the ashram in his absence, he grew furious and demanded an explanation. The head disciple came forward sporting a helpless look and pleaded, 'Guruji, sorry to say this, the ashram cat died in your absence. We tried our level best to find another cat in the neighbourhood to tie to the tree before starting the pooja but couldn't find one until late at night. By the time the search party returned, pooja time was over.'"

What we must keep in mind that the ritual we follow today is a second-hand copy of somebody's work in the past. Our actions should be in the context of our requirements and situation. Spirituality is an 'inside-out' phenomenon, and only a very meagre percentage manages to make any substantial headway with the 'outside-in' approach of ritualism. It is like assuming that by wearing pads, shoes, helmet, gloves, and carrying a bat like Sachin Tendulkar, one will start batting like him. Sounds logical, but there's a lot more that goes into making a batting maestro than meets the eye of the ritualist who would find his stumps flying at the first ball. The point I am trying to make here is that your spiritual quest, meditation techniques, books, soul searching, etc., may look similar to those of many others but will never be the same.

Incompetent Seeker

In the popular Sufi story of 'Laila Majnu', Majnu would run around the village streets of Laila's house, shouting her name and entreating everybody to help him see Laila just once. He would even promise the inhabitants that he would never show his face again if they helped him see her. Tired of his perpetual rants and importuning, the village elders went to meet her father and requested that he allow Majnu a fleeting glimpse of Laila so that they might have some respite from the madman for a few days at least. Laila's father agreed. The villagers arranged a well-lit tent for Laila on top of a sand dune one night and called Majnu to see her after getting the assurance that he would not show his face again in the village. Majnu agreed and was brought at a distance from the tent. As he inched closer to the tent, his heartbeat increased, and he started shivering and sweating. The villagers near the tent got ready to part the curtains of the tent. "Behold!" shouted a village elder. As soon as the curtain parted, Majnu collapsed, unable to withstand a single glimpse of Laila.

Apart from ambition, spirituality requires preparation, too. If the seeker is not competent, he won't be able to withstand the challenges of the journey, however desirous he might be of spiritual growth.

Incompetent Mentor

Rumi has said, "One who follows a fake is, in fact, a fool." From my personal experience, one is ten times more likely to encounter incompetent spiritual gurus than competent ones. What comes as a bigger surprise is that the followers of the incompetent gurus far outnumber those of the competent ones. If such is the case, then how can one identify the real teacher? One sure sign I can share is that the real teacher will not be interested in making you a follower. He will be interested in your growth. And if you are not serious about your own growth, then he will not entertain you beyond a point. He may also expose your ego to test your seriousness or challenge you. He will not be interested in your money, benefits, etc. As Kabir has beautifully put it:

"Sadhu bhookha bhav ka, dhan ka bhookha nahi.
Dhan ka bhookha jo fire, so to sadhu nahi."
(A saint demands that you have faith in what he says, not your money.
He who craves money is not a saint.)

Only a real seeker will be able to associate with and benefit from a real mentor.

Spiritual Ambition

This may come as a surprise to the reader, but spiritual ambition can also become a roadblock on your way to spiritual growth. This is because at the base of ambition usually lies greed which is a characteristic of *nafs*. The following story illustrates this perfectly.

"Mulla Nasruddin goes to a music teacher to learn the violin. He asks the teacher about the fee. The teacher replies, 'It's a six-month course. For the first two months, I will be charging Rs 5,000 per month, and for the next four, Rs 3,000.'

Hearing this, Mulla retorts immediately, 'Can we start from the third month?'"

Most of us get stuck in our spiritual growth because we want to consume spiritual knowledge the way it suits our ego and not in an optimal way. We want to pick up the best spiritual books and join the best spiritual courses without having any idea about our level and growth need. Such people find it beneath them to start their journey with level 1. But by starting with level 2, they will never make it to level 4. Many of the problems that we face in our spiritual quest are not about issues outside us but because of our own orientation and attitude problems.

Food

'You are what you eat' is a universal spiritual wisdom. Sufis also accord this law a lot of value. If one is eating corrupt food, one cannot benefit from spiritual exercises the way an honest man eating lawful food would benefit. A story from the Hindu epic Mahabharata illustrates this.

"After the war of Kurukshetra came to an end, Bhishma (who had been granted a boon that he would die only when he desired) was injured really badly and lay on a bed of arrows. After lying so for fifty-eight days, he decided to wish for death. Before departing from this world, he called both the Kauravas and Pandavas to him. As they stood surrounding him, he gave them some sage advice concerning respect for women and how protecting women was Kshatriya dharma. 'If our own daughters or someone else's daughters (daughters-in-law) are not respected in the house, bad luck is bound to come, and nothing can stop its repercussions.'

Draupadi, the wife of the Pandavas, who was also there in the crowd laughed satirically at this as if questioning where this knowledge of Kshatriya dharma had been when she was being disrobed in the Kaurava court in Bhishma's presence while he helplessly watched.

Bhishma could see her laugh and signalled to her to come closer to him. When she came closer, he said to her, 'My dear daughter, I had this knowledge even then, but as I was eating the evil food of the Kauravas, I could not gather the strength to follow my dharma (duty) to stand up against the Kauravas and protect you. So, my advice to everyone is that if you want to follow your dharma, first and foremost, be watchful of your food.'"

There is also a Biblical legend that prophet Moses could not go and speak freely in the pharaoh's court, despite getting repeated orders from the Lord on Mount Sinai until he stopped eating from the pharaoh's kitchen and fasted for forty days.

Sufism believes in straight path approach to connect with God. Hence, the Sufis advise their disciples to guard their food just as they advise them to guard their thoughts, words, and actions.

Chapter 4

Ready, Get Set, Go

For most of us, thanks to our learning and conditioning, the word spiritual implies the opposite of all that is worldly. Yet this is far from the truth. In fact, spirituality is the art of living in this world without making a mess of our lives. It is the art of mindfully picking and executing the best option in every situation by being your best. It is the art of seeing things as they are. It is the art of seeing the actual reality which is free of our beliefs, illusions, imaginings, prejudices, and fears. Spirituality is seeing the truth with the light of awareness and the refusal to live like a blind person who moves about believing the interpretation of reality fetched to him by his stick. One can also say that spirituality is basking in the glory of the supreme consciousness by feeling, experiencing, and seeing the force that courses through everything that exists in the universe, including us. It is being present to the oneness (non-duality) of all the elements of the universe. It is not about believing somebody's interpretation of it but having the first-hand experience of that reality, the truth.

Before we talk about how to start the spiritual journey, let me explain to the seeker about the sensitive nature of this quest for perfection through the following anecdote.

"Once, a desperate seeker travelled a long distance to meet a popular Sufi of his time. After a long wait, he got to meet the saint. The man greeted the saint and requested that he be accepted as a disciple. The saint refused to initiate him and said, 'You need to have a certain degree of restlessness in you before you can benefit from my teachings.'

A little annoyed with the rejection, the seeker cried out, 'Can't you see that restlessness in me?'

The Sufi replied, 'Yes! I can. But right now you have too much of it.'"

Spiritual work requires a certain mental and emotional capacity before it can be of some benefit to the seeker. By just having aspiration without preparation won't help in one's spiritual growth. In fact, it may prove counterproductive. A sick man will not get the same results from the gym that a healthy man would get. In fact, the exertion would only make him sicker. What the sick person needs before joining a gym is hospitalisation.

In most cases, the spiritual quest begins with a trigger or some dramatic event which forces us to see things beyond our routine thought patterns. This condition creates a unique craving in us for something we may not understand for the lack of familiarity. For years, I mistook creative kicks for spiritual fulfilment. It's these unanswered questions that lead us to probe a little deeper within us.

Though my experience shows that for most of us, introspection is not our first choice. Before this, we try to exhaust our options of googling our questions, watching videos, reading books, joining groups, etc., and only then we get into this zone that is not very familiar to us. To me, this is the beginning of our spiritual odyssey.

Sufism, which is essentially a *bhakti yog* (path of devotion or love) starts with the devotion towards the *sheikh* (guru). The *sheikh* is a living representation of the applied knowledge that the disciple is seeking. He is a perfect example of the 'state of being' that the seeker is aspiring to achieve. No wonder, Sufi *sheikhs* are often referred to as 'live books'. They are difficult to find but not impossible to spot for a serious seeker. The initial journey of a seeker can be broken into the following three steps for the sake of understanding.

1. The first step in this journey is to acknowledge the hunger or craving for fulfilment. A lot of people are so sick that their spiritual hunger has been numbed. As they say, "It's a sick bird that doesn't wish to fly." We are so obsessed with the facilities and cosy life of our mental cages that we have stopped aspiring for flight.
2. The second step is to arrange the resources to prepare food in order to satisfy this hunger. Here, building emotional muscles and

mental capacities is required to push the consciousness of the seeker to the next level. Tools like fasting, meditation, contemplation, reflecting upon scriptures, etc., are very useful at this stage.

3. The third step in the process of satisfying the hunger will be to learn the craft of cooking and consumption of the food. Here we need a person who may give us a live demo of the cooking process; someone who has perfected the art of preparing the food, experimented enough times, and personally undertaken the processes involved in cooking up a delicious meal. Unfortunately, many of us go to chefs (an analogy for gurus) who are either underprepared or have a faulty orientation, and hence, we don't benefit the way we want to. Let me share a story that may help you be present to this issue.

"Once, a serious seeker decided to find a *sheikh*. He enquired from his friends and elders about the characteristics of a true saint . . . their appearance, behaviour, conversation style, etc. Armed with this knowledge, he left home in search of a true saint whom he could adopt as his *sheikh*. He looked at one and all saintly figures closely and tried to gauge their level of saintliness based on the parameters handed to him by his learned friends. This way, he rejected a good number of saints. Finally, one day, while he was standing in the middle of a road, he saw a saint coming towards him. Taking out his 'characteristics-of-a-true-saint' list, he started ticking the boxes. 'Wow!' he exclaimed, 'I have found him!'

By this time, the saint had come quite close. He smiled at him and whispered in his ear, 'Now that you have figured out that I am worthy of being your *sheikh*, let me see whether you are good enough to be my student.'"

A true seeker may learn a thousand lessons from a realised man without even asking a question or even contacting him in person. Imagine how wonderful it would be to have such a person as your mentor. But, as I keep repeating: the magic lies in the student, not the teacher. We will get the wonderful outcomes we aspire for only if we approach these exceptionally talented masters with all our homework done as a worthy *patra* (deserving candidate).

Further Readings

1. *The Forty Rules of Love* by Elif Shafak
2. *The Essential Rumi* by Rumi
3. *The Conference of the Birds* by Attar of Nishapur
4. *The Sufis* by Idries Shah
5. *Mulla Nasruddin Stories* by Idries Shah
6. *Alone with the Alone: Creative Imagination in the Sufism of Ibn 'Arabi* by Henry Corbin
7. *Tales of the Dervishes: Teaching Stories of the Sufi Masters over the Past Thousand Years* by Idries Shah
8. *Me and Rumi: The Autobiography of Shams-i Tabrizi* by Shams-i Tabrizi
9. *Sufism: A Short Introduction* by William C. Chittick
10. *Journey to the Lord of Power: A Sufi Manual on Retreat* by Ibn Arabi
11. *The Divan* by Hafez
12. *The Kashf Al-Mahjub (The Revelation of the Veiled): An Early Persian Treatise on Sufism* by Ali Hujwiri
13. *Learning How to Learn: Psychology and Spirituality in the Sufi Way* by Idries Shah

About the Author

'Brands to Brahm' is how I like to phrase my story. Fifteen years of working in the glitzy and creative world of advertising and searching for fulfilment, I finally managed to find myself while working on the biography of my guru, Hazrat Roshan Shah Warsi.

My spiritual journey started when my mother placed me in the lap of my guru and requested him to bless me with a name. I grew up like any other child in a metropolitan city with the only difference being that I was as comfortable in a mosque as I was in a *satsang*—even at the age of seven.

In the late 1980s and early 1990s, I got many opportunities to spend some memorable summer vacations in my guru's presence. This *sohbet* (company) might have had played a crucial role in shaping my spiritual journey, but frankly speaking, I never realised it then. The rest, as they say, is history.

In 2013, I decided to quit my full-time job and dedicate my second innings to people development and spreading the message of 'conscious living'. I conduct talks and organise workshops and retreats under the banner 'New Age Sufis' to help people gain clarity about their true-self and give them a chance to experience the real transformative power of Sufism, which is a rare thing to find these days.

I am a certified spiritual coach, life coach, NLP, EFT, and L&D professional. I work with corporates as a performance consultant and with individuals as a personal coach.

Mail: hasnainwaris@gmail.com
Website: www.hasnainwaris.com

ACKNOWLEDGEMENTS

I would like to express my gratitude to my uncle Islam and aunty Ayesha for bringing me up as their fifth child and allowing me to attend *satsangs*. To Mushtaq Ahmed, my guru brother, for his 25 years of mentorship that shaped my spiritual quest. To Elham bhai, my brother from another mother, for all his support over the years. To Tabrez, my son, for helping me punch and plan this book. To Shalini Shekhar, Kallol Bhattacherjee, Suma Varughese, Benazir Saheb, Vishal, and Pankhuri for their support and guidance.

I would also like to show my appreciation to Ramakrishna Mission Library, Delhi, where I read all *Amar Chitra Katha* titles on Indian Mythology.

And finally, my salutation to Alampanah Sarkar Haji Waris Ali Shah (R.A.), and my heartfelt gratitude to all the saints and half-saints that I have come across in my journey.

Credits

1. Idries Shah Foundation
2. Jerrahi Order
3. Sufi Comics
4. Wikipedia